ANDY ISID

MW0.601031

GRILL COOKBOOK

for Beginners

The Ultimate Guide
to Learn about Different Types of Grilling,

Tips and Tricks with

100+ YUMMIEST AND HEALTHY
RECIPES

TABLE OF CONTENTS

INTRODUCTION

We are well aware of the fact that grilling and barbeque are a huge part of American culture. Most families have an annual family get-together around the grill with loads of fun and a bit of family drama. Come summer, and everyone is out in their backyard grilling some juicy steak. Almost all homeowners in the United States have at least one grill in their house.

If you have picked up this book, it means that either you are new to grilling and want to learn, or you already grill and want to advance your skills in both cases; this book is perfect for you. This book guides you from the basic guidelines and walks you through the entire experience. Choosing between a gas or charcoal grill is often a difficult decision. In the following chapters, both the styles have been discussed in detail to understand better and eventually make your choice clearer and more accessible. We have in store for you all the information you will be needing to set up your grill, the essential utensils you will be needing, few tricks and tips that will make your food taste even better.

Numerous recipes are included in the book. There are recipes for all occasions, all festivals, and all food groups. Yes, you read it right, for all food groups. When you think of the grill, you assume it is all about meat and seafood, but you are in for a surprise. This book is for everyone and all kinds of foods: meats, vegetables, and even fruits.

All the recipes included in this book are made from simple ingredients which are easy to find. The instructions have been given in a step-by-step fashion so that the recipes are easy to follow. Grilling makes sure that the foods are not as greasy as they are when frying and baking. These recipes are suitable for people who avoid much greasy food but do not want to compromise on the flavors.

5

CHAPTER 1
Introduction to Grilling

We have all heard the term grilling. But do we know exactly what it means? Commonly, we use the words grilling and barbeque interchangeably, but the meanings differ slightly. As a responsible food enthusiast and cook you should always know about the minute details and terms of the food procedures. Some terms like grilling, barbecue and smoking are often used interchangeably but the procedures differ slightly. It also depends on what geographic part of the world you are from. In different countries the same name could mean a slightly different procedure. So, whenever you read a book or recipe, you should always consider where it has been written. This type of context is often useful while understanding different cultures and cuisines.

1.1. Difference Between Grilling and Barbecue

Both grilling and barbecue mean that the food is cooked over an open flame. But there is one fundamental difference, in grilling, the food is cooked on high flame and heat for a shorter period. In contrast, barbecue means cooking on a lower heat level for a more extended period. Another significant difference is that the word barbecue is reserved only for poultry, fish, and meat varieties. In the case of grilling, it is a more inclusive term that also includes fruits and vegetables.

7

Only a person with more knowledge or education about cooking can point out these essential details. Most of the time, these terms mean the same thing. The common point about both methods of cooking is that the food is cooked on a grill.

1.2. Barbecue

It is effortless to get confused between barbecue and grilling. But barbecue is all about slow cooking. The temperatures are often as low as 2000F, and it usually takes a long while, up to several hours. Barbecue is restricted to only meat. The items that are barbecued most often are usually:

- Ribs
- Full turkey
- Beef brisket
- Pork shoulders

The key to a perfect barbecue is to maintain the temperature. This is the tricky part. For a gas grill, it is easy; you turn the gas flame at a low level and leave it to cook. But with the conventional charcoal grill, you will need to add more coals every hour to maintain the temperature. Conventionally barbecue involved smoking the meat, so it is preferred to use charcoal for the barbecue.

1.3. Grilling

If we talk in specific terms, grilling means cooking food short while on a hot flame. A gas grill can use either fuel this cooking, or you can even use charcoal heat. If we give perspective, grilling means getting the food cooked within 30 minutes or less to overheat the 360 OF or more temperature. For thick steaks or mutton chops, the temperature should be raised even further up to 5000F. The increased temperature will ensure a shorter time for cooking. The advantage of grilling is that the meat remains tender and juicy. The key is not to overcook. If the meat is overcooked, it will dry and become chewy and leather-like. Using high temperature will ensure that the heat penetrates the whole meat cut, and a shorter cooking time will prevent the meat from drying out. Some of the meat cuts that are best for grilling are:

- Strip steaks
- Primal cuts
- Ribeye steaks

Thankfully, grilling meats is a relatively simple procedure. You will only have to take care of the temperature and the cooking time. Other than that, meats are typically easy to handle. The same cannot be said about seafood, poultry, and vegetables. More care is required to address these delicate items. As a rule of thumb, meat cuts will require a much higher temperature, around 5000F.

Seafood, chicken fillets, fruits, and vegetable grill at temperatures around 400DF. If you want to grill a whole chicken or pork chops, you will require a much lower temperature of around 300DF.

Now that you know the fundamental difference between grilling and barbecue, we will focus more on grilling: the setup, techniques, and delicious recipes.

CHAPTER 2
Choosing the Correct Grill

Once you have decided that you want to grill, you would require a grill. There are primarily three basic types of grills that are commonly used. In this chapter, we are going to discuss the types. All styles are useful. You have to decide for yourself which one is the most suitable for you. The grill selection depends on what you will use it for and how often it is going to be used. If you are an occasional cook, it is better not to invest too much in a grill but if you plan to grill more often, then investing in a good quality grill is a must.

Once you have decided to purchase a grill, keep in mind that these are not cheap, they are going to cost something. After that, weigh in all the factors that will determine your final decision. Things to consider:

- How often are you going to use it?

- What kind of food are you going to cook?

- Do you have enough storage space for the grill and other equipment?

- Do you have enough open space in your house to have a functioning grill?

11

Answer all these questions honestly and then decide which grill you want in your house. Always go for something reliable and sturdy.

2.1. Types of Grills

We will discuss the three main types of grill here and decide what we want.

1. The Open Grill

This is the primary type of grill we are most familiar with. These are usually made like a metal box which is fitted with a grate. These are typically filled with burning charcoal, and the food is cooked uncovered over the grate. You can even serve this kind of grill with wood for the smoky and aromatic effect. Sometimes the grill has a gas source fitted for higher heating function. This is the standard type of grill. This type of grill is often found in parks as well, the only difference being that at parks, they are permanently fixed and usually have a stone body.

2. Gas Grill with Cover

Gas grills do not use charcoal and use gas as a fuel source. These grills are popular among people because, apart from grilling, they can also be used to roast. Some cooking experts can even bake in a gas grill. This is a practical investment. Using gas is also much more accessible than burning wood and charcoal. The covered gas grill has a cover, and the food can be grilled while being covered as well. This ensures an even temperature and quick cooking.

3. Smoker Grill

The smoker grills are more suitable for significant meat cuts and use the approach where low heat is used for a longer time to tenderize the meat. This grill is mainly used for barbecue and smoking more than grilling. This grill's advantage is the smoky aroma and taste that penetrates the meats and gives a mouth-watering flavour.

2.2. Grill Selection

You must understand that the only way you will be able to grill perfectly is by practice. No matter which grill you buy, it will take time and patience to perfect your technique. So, no grill is the wrong grill. You will have to choose the one that is right for you. As discussed earlier, the decision depends on answering a few questions you need to ask yourself.

1. What kind of food are you going to cook?

Grilling is all about quick and tasty. If you aim to cook food that does not require extensive cooking, you can definitely for the open grill or the gas-covered grill. Both are exceptional. You will be able to make juicy burgers, grill hot dogs, kebabs, chicken fillets, and pork chops. But if you plan to cook significant, juicy meat cuts, which require slow and extensive cooking, you must invest in smoker equipment.

2. How often are you going to use it?

You need to ask yourself this first, what is your main objective? If you plan to use the grill once ir a while or occasionally, then it is better to invest in a primary grill or a gas grill of a small to medium size. If you plan to entertain family and friends, try new flavours, and learn, you should probably invest in something more durable and with multiple functions. A full-size gas grill can be ideal for this situation. The only matter with the gas grill is that the smoky flavour is missing from experience.

3. Do you have space for a grill?

When you are living in a city, space is always an issue. Before making such an investment, analyse how much space the equipment is going to take. Also, consider that you must have enough storage space for the grill and its accompanying equipment when you are not grilling.

CHAPTER 3
Tips and Tricks for Grilling

In this chapter, let us have a look at some tips and tricks for better grilling. Sometimes these tricks prove to be helpful and make your work much more manageable. Following are some guidelines that will make your experience better in more than one way.

3.1. Meats Should not be Frozen

This is one of the most critical lessons everyone should know before grilling. Any meat that hits the grill should be defrosted and be at room temperature. The colder the meat, the longer it will take to cook and the drier it will become. So, the meat must be at room temperature. If you have frozen meat, put it in the refrigerator a night before grilling and take it out of the fridge thirty to forty minutes before grilling so that the meat reaches room temperature. This will ensure cooking of the meats, poultry and seafood properly. Do not miss this step. This is one of the most important and basic steps. If the meats are cold from inside, they will not be thoroughly cooked and the dish will have raw flavor through-out. If it is not raw and you try to grill for too long, this may dry out the meat. In both cases the dish will be spoiled. So, it is better to be careful in the first few steps, rather than spoiling the whole dish.

3.2. Season the Meats Generously

When you grill meats, you should always rub them liberally with seasoning. Always rub the washed meat with salt. The amount of salt should be double compared to the amount of salt used for the same quantity when cooking the conventional way. The spices and peppers should also be generously applied. This has two main advantages; the first, flavors are enhanced. Second, the spices and salt tenderize the raw meat, and the meat takes a shorter while to cook. Proper seasoning ensures the success of the end product. It is the care that you take while the initial steps of cooking that will make your end product perfect. If you do not season your meats and poultry properly, the flavors will not penetrate inside. This will cause the seasoning to be there only on the outside of the meat and the inner parts of the meat will remain bland and tasteless. This is why each step of the process is very important and should be taken into consideration.

3.3. Clean the Grate

Your grill grate should always be clean. Before starting any grilling, see that no residue is left from the previous grilling session. If you use the dirty grill, the meat and other food items will stick to the grate, and turning the food will cause sticking. This step is as important as seasoning and frilling. If you have seasoned and prepared everything properly, and you are great at the grill but the grate is not clean. Although your preparation and technique were perfect but due to a little carelessness in cleaning, you will be headed to spoil the whole dish. This is why, to have a clean grate and grill is essential.

An easy way to clean is while preheating your grill. When the grill grate is heated, use a large brush to clean the grate and then use oil dipped kitchen towels to wipe the grate, holding them with a pair of tongs. If you do the cleaning and maintenance of your equipment regularly, the task will seem easier. In the same way if you delay cleaning your utensils and equipment, more dirt will deposit on the equipment and will become more and more difficult to clean and maintain.

3.4. Preheat the Grill

It's always a good idea to properly preheat your grill. As for baking, preheating the oven is essential; for perfect grilling, preheating is equally crucial. For a medium heated grill, preheat for at least twenty to thirty minutes. For a hot temperature, preheat for forty minutes. Another advantage of preheating is that it has natural anti-bacterial effects.

3.5. Create Heat Sections

This is a pro tip. No one will tell you this. The meat needs high heat to start cooking, but the meat does not require high heat rather than medium heat to let it cook without burning. An intelligent technique with a double gas burner grill would be to put one burner on high flame and the other burner on medium flame. Start the cooking on the high side and transfer the food to the other side towards the end. Similarly, for a charcoal grill, put all the charcoal towards the center to create a heat center and move the food towards the sides when the food needs lower heat.

3.6. Do not Move and Stab the Meat

Now, when you put the meat on the grill, please wait for it to form a light cooked crust in the meat layer before turning it. If you turn it in before the crust is created, the meat will stick to the grill. Another thing you should refrain from doing is; do not poke the meat to check for doneness. This will cause the meat juices to release and make the meat dry. Dry meat becomes chewy and is deprived of the juicy and fresh flavor. Always use the correct equipment to move around food items on the grill. Never let your hands near the grate; use a tong or spatula instead.

3.7. Use Skewers

If you are running short on time, the best trick is to cut the meat and thread it to skewers. By cutting the meat into smaller pieces, you will increase the surface area, and thus the cooking will be accelerated. Another advantage of using skewers is that they help meats that shrink and curl when heat is applied. This technique is best for chicken and shrimps that lose shape after being exposed to heat. Another important consideration is that the pieces should be threaded with a bit of space between them. Otherwise, the details will not be cooked all the way. People usually make one more mistake by putting meat and veggies in the same skewers; this doesn't seem right. In such cases, the veggies start burning from the edges, and the meat is not even nearly done. Veggies and meat should always be on separate skewers.

3.8. Do not Marinate Meat with Sauce

Another essential tip is not to marinate the meat in a saucy marinate. Often, we use sauce with grilled meats, but the trick is to add the sauce only towards the end of grilling. Just one minute before taking the meat off the grill, brush the sauce over the meats. If you add the sauce earlier, it might stick to the grate, especially if the sauce is sweet.

3.9. Do not Overcook

This should be considered very seriously. Food keeps on cooking for around 3 to 4 minutes even after being taken off the grill. So, it is always a good idea to take off the food before it is fully cooked. Overcooked food loses its flavor as well as becomes dry and difficult to eat.

3.10. Give the Meat Rest

As soon as you take the food off the grill, do not start serving. Let the meat rest for 3 to 5 minutes before slicing and consuming. These 5 minutes allow the meat to cook thoroughly and the meat juices to be settled back into the meat.

3.11. Clean the Grill

Cleanliness is essential for cooking—especially grilling. Whenever you examine, there are residue and food particles attached to the grill. While the grill is still hot, remove the residue with a stiff brush and an oil-dipped paper towel. Always use tongs to handle the paper tower, and never put your hands directly near the grill.

CHAPTER 4
Appetizers and Salads

This chapter includes delicious grilled recipes for starters and salads. Appetizers are very popular while dining out. But in recent times it is mostly encouraged to prepare your own food and dine out only when it is necessary. But, eating at home should not mean that we always consume conventional food. We can also trat ourselves with a high quality experience. In this chapter, you will find simple yet delicious recipes that will bring the restaurant experience home for you.

4.1. Asparagus Salad

TOTAL TIME
40'

PREPARATION TIME
35'

COOK TIME
5'

SERVING
35

COURSE
SALAD

COUSINE
AMERICAN

The first recipe in this chapter is delicious as well as healthy. Asparagus is known to be rich in vitamins and has detoxifying effect. This salad is light on the stomach and gives you a fresh experience. This is one of the best options for a warm sunny summer day.

INGREDIENTS

- ½ kg asparagus
- ½ tsp pepper
- 3 cups mesclun
- ½ tsp salt
- 1 cup cherry tomatoes
- 4 tbsp orange juice
- 200g cheddar cheese cut in small cubes
- 1 cup cooked chickpeas
- ½ cup olives coarsely chopped
- 2 tsp mustard
- 1 tbsp vinegar
- 1 tbsp lemon juice
- ½ cup olive oil
- 1 medium cucumber diced

DIRECTIONS

1. First, preheat the grill for 10 to 15 minutes so that medium heat is achieved.
2. Mix some oil with salt and pepper and rub the mixture on the asparagus generously.
3. Grill for five minutes on the heated grill, turning and tossing in between. Make sure the asparagus becomes tender and cooked but not burnt.
4. Take out on a plate, let it cool for 2 minutes, and then cut into 1 ½ inch pieces.
5. In a large salad bowl, mix the asparagus with mesclun, halved cherry tomatoes, cucumbers, cheese, olives, and chickpeas.
6. Now prepare the dressing. In a bowl, mix the orange juice, vinegar, and lemon juice. Whisk it and add the mustard. Mix properly and then add the remaining olive oil and whisk thoroughly. Drizzle the dressing on the salad and serve.

4.2. Plum Salad with Walnuts

TOTAL TIME
30'

PREPARATION TIME
20'

COOK TIME
10'

SERVING
4

COURSE
SALAD

COUSINE
AMERICAN

This salad is a wonderful mix of fruit, leafy greens and nuts. All these three components are packed with vitamins and give your immunity a boast. The walnuts are a great source of omega 3 fatty acids which are essential for the brain and protect it against many neurodegenerative diseases. So, this salad is a must if you want a healthy mind and body.

INGREDIENTS

- 750 g plums
- 1 medium lettuce head
- 100g blue cheese
- ½ tsp salt
- ½ tsp sugar
- 50 g fresh basil leaves
- ½ cup walnuts
- 4 tbsp olive oil
- 2 tbsp vinegar

DIRECTIONS

1. Preheat the grill for 20 minutes so that it reaches medium heat.
2. Prepare the plums by pitting them and cutting them in half. Rub the plums with very little olive oil.
3. Next, put the plums on the grill with the skin side down. Let it grill for 3 to 4 minutes till plums start to caramelize and the grill marks are formed. Flip over the plums and grill for one more minute.
4. Take the plums of the flame and let them rest.
5. In a pan, toast the walnuts for one to two minutes. Take care that the walnuts are not burnt.
6. Prepare the salad dressing. Whisk the balsamic salt with olive oil. Whisk thoroughly.
7. Now, in a large salad bowl, tear the lettuce into smaller pieces. Add the basil leaves, and then add the plums and walnuts. Toss the salad and add the blue cheese to the end.
8. Drizzle with the dressing and enjoy your salad.

4.3. Grilled Apricot Salad

TOTAL TIME
30'

PREPARATION TIME
20'

COOK TIME
5'

SERVING
4

COURSE
SALAD

COUSINE
AMERICAN

This apricot salad is packed with flavour and energy. You can have it as an appetizer and even as a light lunch option. It is a combination of fruits and nuts which will give you an immunity boost. The almonds will give your mind calm and energy to carry through the day. The cheese will melt in your mouth making your experience all worthwhile.

INGREDIENTS

- 750 g apricots
- 1 medium lettuce head
- 100g blue cheese
- ½ tsp salt
- ½ tsp sugar
- 50 g fresh basil leaves
- ¾ cup almonds
- 4 tbsp olive oil
- 2 tbsp vinegar

DIRECTIONS

1. Preheat the grill for 20 minutes so that it reaches medium heat.
2. Prepare the apricots by pitting them and cutting them in half. Rub the apricots with very little olive oil.
3. Next, put the apricots on the grill with the skin side down. Let it grill for 3 to 4 minutes till the apricots start to caramelize and the grill marks are formed. Flip over the apricots and grill for one more minute.
4. Take the apricots of the flame and let them rest.
5. In a pan, toast the almonds for one to two minutes. Take care that the almonds are not burnt.
6. Prepare the salad dressing. Whisk the balsamic salt with olive oil. Whisk thoroughly.
7. Now, in a large salad bowl, tear the lettuce into smaller pieces. Add the basil leaves, and then add the grilled apricots and toasted almonds. Top the salad with blue cheese
8. Drizzle with the dressing and serve after refrigeration.

4.4. Grilled Peach Salad

TOTAL TIME
30'

PREPARATION TIME
20'

COOK TIME
5'

SERVING
4

COURSE
SALAD

COUSINE
AMERICAN

This is another amazing salad packed with vitamins and anti-oxidants. This salad is a good option for your body detox. The pine nuts and the soft crumbly goat cheese make this experience mouth-watering. Once you try this recipe, you will be coming back for it again and again. Try this recipe and you will not regret.

INGREDIENTS

- 1 kg peaches
- 1 medium lettuce head
- 100g soft goat cheese
- ½ tsp salt
- ½ tsp sugar
- ¼ cup raisins
- ½ cup pine nuts
- ½ cup olive oil
- 5 tbsp vinegar

DIRECTIONS

1. Preheat the grill for 20 minutes so that it reaches medium heat.
2. Prepare the peaches by pitting them and cutting them into four pieces. Rub the peaches with very little olive oil.
3. Next, put the peaches on the grill with the skin side down. Let it grill for 3 to 4 minutes till the peaches start to caramelize and the grill marks are formed. Flip over the peaches and grill for one more minute.
4. Take the fruit of the flame and let them rest.
5. In a pan, toast the pine nuts for one to two minutes. Take care that the nuts are not burnt.
6. Prepare the salad dressing. Whisk the balsamic salt with olive oil. Whisk thoroughly.
7. Now, in a large salad bowl, tear the lettuce into smaller pieces. Add the raisins, and then add the grilled peaches and toasted pine nuts. Top the salad with soft goat cheese.
8. Drizzle with the dressing and enjoy your salad.

4.5. Mixed Veggie Salad

TOTAL TIME
40'

PREPARATION TIME
30'

COOK TIME
10'

SERVING
3-4

COURSE
SALAD

COUSINE
AMERICAN

This salad is like comfort food for the vegetarian soul. This salad recipe makes a heavenly bowl of delicious vegetables all coming together to give great flavours. If you are someone who loves vegetables, this one is just for you. Along with its mouth-watering flavours, it is packed with vitamins and anti-oxidants. Vegetables are the best health food. Even if you are not that fond of vegetables, you can make this salad as a side dish for your main meals.

INGREDIENTS

- 2 eggplants
- 1 large onion
- 1 large zucchini
- 1 red bell pepper
- 1 yellow bell pepper
- ¼ tsp salt
- ½ tsp pepper
- ½ cup olive oil
- ½ tsp grated garlic
- 2 tbsp vinegar
- 1 tsp lemon juice

DIRECTIONS

1. Preheat the grill for 15 minutes.
2. Cut all the vegetables in slices or diced. Drizzle oil on the vegetables and rub the oil on the surface. Arrange all the vegetables on skewers.
3. Grill the vegetables for 2 minutes on each size and set them aside.
4. Let the vegetables rest and meanwhile make the dressing.
5. Mix the salt pepper, remaining olive oil, vinegar, lemon juice and, garlic. Mix well.
6. In a large salad bowl, toss all the vegetables and drizzle with dressing.
7. Enjoy your salad with plain or spicy fried rice.

4.6. Sweet Potato Salad

TOTAL TIME
1 HOUR

PREPARATION TIME
10'

COOK TIME
50'

SERVING
8

COURSE
SALAD

COUSINE
AMERICAN

This is one recipe that is very much in trend these days. Everyone is trying sweet potato recipes. This recipe gives the sweet potato a different taste profile. You do not come across grilled sweet potato very often. It is mostly sweet potato chips or crisps. This recipe gives you grilled sweet potatoes with mushrooms and scallions which enhance the already high flavour profile. This is one recipe you should definitely try.

INGREDIENTS

- 4 large sweet potatoes
- ½ cup olive oil
- 8 scallions
- 2 tsp mustard
- 1 tsp honey
- ¼ tsp salt
- ¼ tsp pepper
- 2 tbsp apple cider vinegar
- 1 tbsp vinegar
- ¼ cup freshly chopped parsley

DIRECTIONS

1. Preheat oven to 400°F.
2. Wash the sweet potatoes and put them in a baking tray, and bake for 45 minutes.
3. Next, preheat the grill.
4. Please take out the potatoes from the oven, peel them and chop them into 1 ½ inch pieces.
5. Now put the potatoes and the scallions on the grill.
6. The scallions take very little time to grill. Only one minute on each side and them take out on a plate.
7. The potatoes take longer. 5 minutes on each side.
8. Take the potatoes off from the grill and let them rest for 5 minutes.
9. Meanwhile, prepare the salad dressing.
10. Mix all the remaining ingredients except for parsley to form a dressing.
11. In a large bowl, put in the scallions, potatoes, and parsley.
12. Drizzle the dressing and enjoy your salad.

4.7. Potato Salad

TOTAL TIME
50'

PREPARATION TIME
10'

COOK TIME
40'

SERVING
6

COURSE
SALAD

COUSINE
AMERICAN

Potatoes are our all-time favourite comfort food. Nothing gives our tummy satisfaction like the good old potatoes. This recipe is no exception. Although the name suggests that it is a salad, but deep inside we all know that his is our comfort food. You know you will be coming back for the potato salad.

INGREDIENTS

- 5 potatoes
- ½ cup olive oil
- 2 red onions
- 1 tsp mustard
- 1 tsp honey
- ¼ tsp salt
- ¼ tsp pepper
- 2 tbsp lemon juice
- 1 tbsp vinegar
- ¼ cup freshly chopped cilantro

- 100g cheddar cheese cubed

DIRECTIONS

1. Preheat oven to 3500F.
2. Wash the potatoes and put them in a baking tray, and bake for 40 minutes.
3. Next, preheat the grill.
4. Please take out the potatoes from the oven, peel them and chop them into 1 ½ inch pieces. Cover them with a little olive oil.
5. Now put the potatoes on the grill.
6. Grill the potatoes for 5 minutes on each side and take them off the grill to rest for 5 minutes. This helps the potatoes to retain firmness. If you toss the salad when the potatoes are still very warm, the potatoes might crumble.
7. Cut the onions and thread them on skewers. Drizzle some oil on the onions. Grill the onions one minute on each side and take them off the grill. Let them rest.
8. Meanwhile, prepare the salad dressing.
9. Mix the olive oil, lemon juice, vinegar, and mustard. Whisk it well till the oil is emulsified.
10. In a large bowl, put in the onions, potatoes, cilantro, and cheese.
11. Drizzle the dressing and enjoy your salad.

4.8. Zucchini Salad with Aromatic Herbs

TOTAL TIME
40'

PREPARATION TIME
20'

COOK TIME
20'

SERVING
4

COURSE
SALAD

COUSINE
AMERICAN

This is a highly nutritious salad. This is full of vitamins and anti-oxidants. This is the ultimate healthy salad. Try out this salad and you will be coming back for more again and again.

INGREDIENTS

- 2 large zucchinis
- 2 large leeks
- ½ cup walnuts
- 2 garlic cloves grated
- ½ cup fresh parsley
- ¼ tsp salt
- ¼ tsp pepper
- 2 tbsp lemon juice
- ¼ cup olive oil

DIRECTIONS

1. Preheat the grill for 20 minutes to get medium to high heat.
2. Cut the half of the zucchini lengthwise and set them aside.
3. Cut the leeks so that you get the white and the light green part. Cut them lengthwise. Some parts of the root should still be attached.
4. In a pan, toast the walnuts for about 5 minutes till an aroma is released. Take them off the pan and on a cutting board. Chop the walnuts coarsely.
5. Put the walnuts in a salad bowl and add garlic, 2 tbsp oil, lemon juice, pepper, and salt. Toss all the ingredients.
6. Next, brush some olive oil on the zucchini and leeks. Put the vegetables on the grill.
7. Turn them after every one or two minutes. Taking care that they don't burn. It usually takes five minutes for the leeks to be done. It takes longer for zucchini, around ten minutes.
8. After the grilling, put the vegetables on the cutting board and let them s=rest for one or two minutes.
9. Next, remove the roots from the leeks and chop them coarsely. Add these to the salad bowl.
10. Cut the zucchini into one-inch pieces and put it in the salad bowl.
11. Toss the salad and enjoy it with family and friends.

4.9. Grilled Eggplant and Kale Salad

TOTAL TIME
35'

PREPARATION TIME
20'

COOK TIME
15'

SERVING
4

COURSE
SALAD

COUSINE
AMERICAN

INGREDIENTS

- 2 medium round eggplants
- 2 large bunches of kale
- 1 tsp turmeric powder
- ¼ cup olive oil
- ½ cup fresh mint leaves
- 1 cup Greek yogurt
- 1 lemon
- ½ tsp curry powder
- ¼ tsp salt
- ¼ tsp pepper

DIRECTIONS

1. Preheat the grill for about 20 minutes to get medium to high heat.
2. Cut the eggplant into thick slices.
3. In a large bowl, add turmeric, 2 tbsp olive oil, pepper, and salt. Whisk the ingredients.
4. Toss the eggplant slices in the turmeric mixture.
5. Now grill the eggplant slices. Two minutes on each side, take them off the grill and rest for 5 minutes.
6. Next, grill the kale bunches.
7. Grill around one minute on each side and grill till light marks of the grill appear on the leaves.
8. Take them off the grill and onto a cutting board. Chop the kale into bite-sized pieces. Chop off the roots.
9. In a large salad bowl, mix the eggplant, kale leaves, mint leaves and, olive oil. Toss them together.
10. In another bowl, mix the yogurt and curry powder. Drizzle the yogurt over the eggplant and kale salad.
11. Top it with a little olive oil and lemon wedges.

4.10. Bread Salad

TOTAL TIME
30'

PREPARATION TIME
15'

COOK TIME
15'

SERVING
4

COURSE
SALAD

COUSINE
AMERICAN

Who does not like bread? There must be very few people in the world who would not be fond of bread. In this recipe we have turned the bread into a salad. You will surely enjoy this twist. This salad is purely a feel good salad and you will be coming back for this salad again and again.

INGREDIENTS

- ½ loaf of freshly baked bread
- 3 tbsp vinegar
- 2 red onions
- ¼ cup olive oil
- 2 red bell peppers
- ¼ tsp salt
- ¼ tsp pepper
- ½ tsp paprika
- 3 tsp chopped chives

DIRECTIONS

1. Remove the crusts of the bread and tear the bread into large pieces with your hands.
2. Preheat the grill to get medium to high heat.
3. Peel the onions while the root is attached and quarter it with the root intact.
4. Cut the bell peppers in half and remove the seeds.
5. In a small bowl, add 2 tbsp of oil and a pinch of salt and pepper. Mix it and toss the bread in this.
6. In another bowl, add 2 tbsp of oil and a pinch of salt and pepper. Mix and toss the bell peppers and onions.
7. Next, grill the bread pieces, occasionally turning them. It takes around 5 to 8 minutes. Take care that you don't burn the bread.
8. When the bread is done, take off the grill onto a plate.
9. Now, grill the onions and bell peppers. Grilling for around 2 minutes on each side.
10. Next, put the onions and bell peppers on the cutting board. Remove the root from the onions and separate the layers.
11. Remove the skin of the bell peppers and chop coarsely.
12. In a large salad bowl, toss the bread, peppers, onion, and chives. Drizzle some olive oil on the salad. Top with salt, pepper, and a bit of vinegar.

4.11. Mushroom and Carrot Salad

TOTAL TIME
30'

PREPARATION TIME
15'

COOK TIME
15'

SERVING
4

COURSE
SALAD

COUSINE
AMERICAN

This is a delicious salad, full of nutrition and vitamins. Mushrooms are a great source of protein and energy and carrots are great source of vitamins. Both these components are essential for the proper functioning of your body. You should at least include one nutritious salad in your daily intake of food. This hearty salad should make the cut to your favourite salads.

INGREDIENTS

- 100g shiitake mushrooms
- 500g maitake mushrooms
- 250g small carrots
- ¼ tsp salt
- ¼ tsp ground black pepper
- 6 tbsp olive oil
- 2tsp toasted sesame seeds
- 1 tsp grated ginger
- 3 scallions thinly sliced
- 2 tbsp vinegar
- 2 tbsp thick soy sauce
- 1 tbsp sesame oil

DIRECTIONS

1. Prepare the grill. Preheat it for medium to high heat.
2. Cut the carrots into half lengthwise.
3. In a large bowl, add 3 tbsp olive oil, salt, and pepper.
4. Toss the mushrooms and carrots in the bowl till they are coated with a light layer of oil.
5. Next, grill the mushrooms and carrots.
6. Mushrooms take around 5 minutes to grill. While grilling, keep turning the sides so that the mushrooms do not burn.
7. For carrots, grill for 3 to 4 minutes on each side.
8. Take off the vegetables from the grill and let them rest.
9. Prepare the dressing in a large salad bowl. Whisk together 2 tbsp of olive oil, sesame oil, vinegar, and ginger.
10. Add the scallions and sesame seeds to the dressing.
11. Chop the mushrooms and carrots into bite-sized pieces and add to the salad bowl.
12. Toss the ingredients together and enjoy your meal.

4.12. Crouton Salad

TOTAL TIME
20'

PREPARATION TIME
10'

COOK TIME
10'

SERVING
4

COURSE
SALAD

COUSINE
AMERICAN

This salad again is an example of a comfort food salad. There are times in our lives when nothing can cure us but our favourite comfort foods. This salad is for such times. Apart from being a comfort food it has high content of protein which is essential for your bone and muscle health.

INGREDIENTS

- 10 cherry tomatoes
- 1 bunch scallions
- ¼ cup olive oil
- 4 slices bread
- 1 garlic clove
- ¼ tsp salt
- ¼ tsp pepper
- 2 cups arugula
- 2 tbsp vinegar

DIRECTIONS

1. Prepare the grill for medium to high heat.
2. In a small bowl, toss the scallions in 2 tbsp oil, salt, and pepper.
3. Grill the scallions. 2 minutes on each side.
4. Do not overheat. Be careful not to burn the scallions.
5. Next, remove the crusts of the bread slices and brush them with oil on both sides. Grill the bread slices for two minutes on each side.
6. Grate the garlic cloves and then rub them on both sides of the bread.
7. Tear the bread slices into pieces and put them in a large salad bowl.
8. Chop the scallions and add to the salad bowl.
9. Add all the remaining ingredients to the salad bowl and toss.

4.13. Grilled Lettuce with Pita

TOTAL TIME
20'

PREPARATION TIME
5'

COOK TIME
15'

SERVING
4

COURSE
SALAD

COUSINE
AMERICAN

This salad is a wonderful combination of freshness and flavour. This salad is a best fit for a warm summer day. This salad is high in vitamins and detoxifying ingredients. The rich flavours will make you come back for more.

INGREDIENTS

- 8 heads of small Gem Lettuce
- 1 cup cherry tomatoes halved
- ¼ cup olive oil
- 4 pita pieces of bread
- ¼ tsp salt
- ¼ tsp pepper
- 2 tbsp chopped tarragon
- 1 red onion chopped
- 1 tsp mustard
- 5o g ricotta cheese

- ½ cup fresh chopped parsley

DIRECTIONS

1. Preheat the grill for 20 minutes to get medium to high heat.
2. In a large bowl, add 2 tbsp olive oil, salt, and pepper. Toss the lettuce in this mixture.
3. Tear the pitas along the seams. Then brush with olive oil on both sides.
4. Grill the pitas. One minute on each side and then take them off the grill. Let them rest for a while, then tear them into bite-sized pieces.
5. Grill the lettuce. 2 minutes on each side. Remove from the grill and let it rest for 2 to 3 minutes.
6. Then, separate the leaves of the lettuce.
7. In a large salad bowl, add the chopped onion, vinegar, mustard, olive oil, and tarragon. Whisk together.
8. Next, add the lettuce, tomatoes, cheese, parsley, and then pita.
9. Toss the ingredients together.
10. Enjoy the salad.

4.14. Grilled Fruit Salad

TOTAL TIME
30'

PREPARATION TIME
10'

COOK TIME
20'

SERVING
6

COURSE
SALAD

COUSINE
AMERICAN

When you think about fruits, freshness comes to your mind. This salad is no exception. This fruit salad is a bowl full of heavenly freshness and great flavour. The flavour of fruits is enhanced because of grilling. Grilling makes the fruit sugars caramelize and give an amazing aroma and a distinctly delicious flavour.

INGREDIENTS

- 4 corn ears
- 2 nectarines cut into wedges
- 1 onion thinly sliced
- 100g Cotija cheese
- 1 cup basil leaves
- ¼ tsp ground black pepper
- ¼ tsp salt
- ¼ tsp cumin
- ½ tsp chili powder
- ½ cup olive oil

- 4 tbsp lemon juice
- ½ tsp coriander seeds
- 1 tsp fresh rosemary
- 1 tsp hot sauce

DIRECTIONS

1. Preheat the grill for 20 minutes for medium to high heat.
2. Next, brush the corn ears with 2 tbsp of olive oil and season with salt and chili powder.
3. Grill the corn ears. Around 5 minutes on each side. Press the corns to check for doneness. If still not soft, grill for additional 2 minutes on each side. Take off from the grill and let it rest. After 5 minutes, remove all the kernels from the cob and set them aside in a bowl.
4. In a pan, toast the cumin and coriander seeds while constantly stirring. Toast for 2 to 3 minutes. Wait for the spices to cool and then grind in a spice machine.
5. In a large salad bowl, add lemon juice, the spice mix, hot sauce. 4 tbsp olive oil, rosemary, salt, and pepper. Whisk thoroughly.
6. Add to this dressing the corn kernels, sliced onion, crumbled cheese, nectarines, and basil leaves.
7. Toss all the ingredients and enjoy your salad.

4.15. Grilled Cinnamon Apples

TOTAL TIME
20'

PREPARATION TIME
15'

COOK TIME
5'

SERVING
4

COURSE
SALAD

COUSINE
AMERICAN

This is delicious and healthy. Apples are a great source of iron and vitamins. Cinnamon also has its herbal qualities. It is good for the sour throat and cinnamon is an antiseptic and antioxidant. This is a simple recipe to follow and is liked among kids and adults alike.

INGREDIENTS

- 4 ripe apples
- 3 tbsp olive oil
- 2 tsp honey
- ¼ tsp cinnamon powder
- 2 tsp lemon juice
- 2 tsp orange juice

DIRECTIONS

1. Preheat the grill for 10 minutes for low to medium heat.
2. Cut each apple into four pieces and remove the seeds.
3. Brush the apples with 1 tbsp olive oil.
4. Put the apples on the grill and grill for 1 to 2 minutes on each side. Let the apple caramelize.
5. Take off the apples from the grill and let them rest.
6. Meanwhile, make a dressing. Whisk the lemon juice, orange juice, olive oil, and cinnamon powder to make a smooth dressing.
7. Next, set the grilled apples on a large serving plate and drizzle with the dressing.

4.16. Pineapple and Walnut Salad

TOTAL TIME
20'

PREPARATION TIME
15'

COOK TIME
5'

SERVING
4

COURSE
SALAD

COUSINE
AMERICAN

This is another salad which is packed with vitamins and energy. The pineapple is a source of vitamin C and it is good for your immunity. Similarly, the walnuts are good for your brain health. When you eat this dish, the softness of the pineapple against the crunchiness of the walnut makes it a winning combination.

INGREDIENTS

- 1 pineapple
- ½ cup walnuts
- 1 head romaine lettuce
- 2 tbsp olive oil
- ¼ tsp cayenne pepper
- 2 tsp pineapple juice
- ¼ tsp salt

DIRECTIONS

1. Preheat the grill for 5 to 10 minutes for low heat.
2. Cut the pineapple and form thick rings.
3. Brush the pineapple rings with 1 tbsp olive oil and put them on the grill.
4. Grill for 1 minute on each side and take them off the grill. Let the pineapple rings rest, and then chop them coarsely.
5. In a pan, toast the walnuts for 2 minutes till the nutty aroma is released. Let the walnuts cool, and then chop them coarsely.
6. In a large salad bowl, whisk the dressing.
7. Add 2 tbsp olive oil, cayenne pepper, pineapple juice, and salt. Whisk them thoroughly.
8. Next, tear the romaine lettuce leaves into bite-sized pieces and put them in the salad bowl.
9. Add to this bowl the walnuts and pineapples.
10. Toss them well and enjoy your salad.

4.17. Grilled Squash Salad

TOTAL TIME
20'

PREPARATION TIME
10'

COOK TIME
10'

SERVING
4

COURSE
SALAD

COUSINE
AMERICAN

This is a simple salad you can make as a side dish or even if you are a vegetarian, you can eat it separately. The good thing about this salad is that it is a complete meal. You will not be needing anything accompanying this salad, this is amazing on its own. Apart from being delicious, this salad is packed with vitamins that are essential for your immune response and overall physical wellbeing.

INGREDIENTS

- ½ kg summer squash
- 2 cups mesclun
- ½ onion thinly sliced
- ½ cup crumbled feta cheese
- ¼ cup olive oil
- 4 tbsp vinegar
- ¼ tsp salt
- ¼ pepper

DIRECTIONS

1. Preheat the grill for 10 minutes for medium heat level.
2. In a large bowl, add the vinegar and sliced onion. Let the onion sit for 5 minutes. Next, add the salt and pepper. Mix well in the end whisk in 2 tbsp olive oil.
3. Next, cut the squash into thick slices or wedges (according to your preference.
4. Now, brush olive oil on the squash and season with salt and pepper.
5. Grill for 3 to 4 minutes on each side.
6. Let the grilled squash rest, and then toss it inside the salad bowl with the onion.
7. Next, add the mesclun and top with crumbled feta cheese.
8. Enjoy your delicious salad.

4.18. Vegetable Salad with Rice

TOTAL TIME
30'

PREPARATION TIME
15'

COOK TIME
15'

SERVING
5

COURSE
SALAD

COUSINE
AMERICAN

This is a salad and can also be consumed as a main dish with a side of rice. The vegetables in this recipe are packed with vitamins and are excellent for your immune response and overall health. If you are someone who practices vegetarianism, this is a perfect way of life and you will love to eat this salad with rice since it can be eaten as a main course as well.

INGREDIENTS

- 150 g okra
- ½ cup shredded coconut
- ¼ cup olive oil
- 3 corn ears
- 2 large zucchinis
- 3 large red chilis
- 1 tsp salt
- 1 large eggplant
- 2 garlic cloves minced
- 1 tbsp lime juice

- ¼ cup chopped cilantro
- ¼ cup torn basil
- ¼ cup fennel fronds
- ¼ cup chopped mint leaves
- ¼ cup tarragon
- 2 tbsp fish sauce
- 1 tsp brown sugar
- 3 cups jasmine rice

DIRECTIONS

1. Preheat the grill for 10 minutes for medium to high heat levels.
2. Next, preheat the oven at 250F. Line a baking tray with butter paper, spread coconut on the tray, and bake for 10 minutes. Set aside.
3. Next, prepare the vegetables. Cut the zucchinis in half lengthwise and take out the center.
4. Cut the eggplant into one-inch slices lengthwise.
5. In a large bowl, mix all the vegetables except the chilis. Add 2 tbsp oil and ¼ tsp salt. Toss them well so that all vegetables have a thin layer of olive oil on them.
6. Next, arrange all the vegetables on the grill. Keep flipping the vegetables and grill for around 8 to 10 minutes.
7. Separately, grill chilis for one minute on each side and set them aside.
8. Let the vegetables rest. Remove the corn kernels from the corn cobs and put them in a large salad bowl.
9. Cut the zucchini into bite-size pieces. Could you put them in the bowl with the corn?
10. Next, cut the tops of the okras and cut them into two pieces lengthwise. Mix with other vegetables in a salad bowl.
11. Next, remove the skin from the grilled chilis. Puree these chilis with seeds and mix with the grated garlic. Add sugar and use a pestle and mortar to create a mixture. Put in a small bowl and whisk in the lime juice and fish sauce.
12. Now, drizzle this dressing on the veggie salad and top with baked coconut.
13. Serve with steamed white rice.

37

4.19. Ratatouille Salad

TOTAL TIME
45'

PREPARATION TIME
30'

COOK TIME
15'

SERVING
4

COURSE
SALAD

COUSINE
AMERICAN

Another amazing and delicious recipe. This salad is full of vitamins and nutrition. You should this recipe. This salad goes well with a lot of other beef and chicken dishes. The texture of the grilled eggplant and tomatoes make the overall dish worth a try.

INGREDIENTS

- 200 g tomatoes
- 2 eggplants
- ½ kg summer squash
- 1 red bell pepper
- 6 scallions
- 2 tbsp vinegar
- 4 tbsp olive oil
- ¼ tsp salt
- ¼ tsp pepper
- 1 tbsp chopped tarragon

DIRECTIONS

1. Prepare the grill for a medium to high heat setting.
2. Cut the eggplants lengthwise and rub them with salt on the white side. Let it sit for 10 minutes and then wash and pat dry.
3. Cut the squash lengthwise into half.
4. Next, brush all the vegetables with olive oil and season with salt and pepper.
5. Grill all vegetables with occasional flipping and turning. All the vegetables take around 5 to 8 minutes to grill. The tomatoes and scallions will be grilled within 5 minutes so take them off the frill first.
6. The squash, eggplant, and bell pepper would require around 8 minutes to cook.
7. Slice half of the tomatoes in half and remove the skins. Mash them with a masher and put them in a medium bowl. Add vinegar and 2 tbsp olive oil and whisk well. Season with salt and pepper. This is the salad dressing.
8. Chop the remaining half of the tomatoes and put them in a large bowl. Chop all the other vegetables into small 1-inch pieces and transfer to the same bowl. Drizzle with the dressing and toss well. Top with tarragon.

4.20. Apple and Peach Nutty Salad

TOTAL TIME
25'

PREPARATION TIME
15'

COOK TIME
10'

SERVING
2

COURSE
SALAD

COUSINE
AMERICAN

This fruit salad is delicious fresh and full of energy. This salad is exactly what you want on a warm summer day. This boosts up your energy and the sweet caramelized peaches hit the perfect flavour notes. Apart from being delicious this salad is a great brain food because of the nuts. Nuts are great for your brain health and fruits are an amazing source of vitamins. So, this salad is something you should definitely not miss.

INGREDIENTS

- 1 ripe apple
- 2 peaches
- ¼ tsp cinnamon
- 1 tsp honey
- 2 tsp lemon juice
- ½ cup walnuts
- 1 tbsp olive oil

DIRECTIONS

1. Preheat the gril for 10 minutes for low to medium heat level.
2. Cut the apple into 6 pieces cut lengthwise. Remove the seeds.
3. Pit the peach and cut them into 4 pieces each.
4. Grill the peach pieces first. Grill the peach for 2 minutes on each side. Take off the grill and set aside.
5. Similarly, grill the apples. The only difference is to grill for 2 to 3 minutes on each side
6. Let the fruits rest for 2 minutes, and then chop them coarsely.
7. In a pan, toast the walnuts for 2 minutes and transfer to a salad bowl.
8. A smaller bowl prepares the dressing by whisking together the oil, lime juice, honey, and cinnamon powder.
9. Add the fruits to the salad bowl where the walnuts are already places. Toss together and drizzle with the dressing.
10. Enjoy your salad.

39

4.21. Grilled Apple and Spinach Salad

TOTAL TIME
30'

PREPARATION TIME
15'

COOK TIME
15'

SERVING
2-3

COURSE
SALAD

COUSINE
AMERICAN

This is one salad which you should definitely try. This had a simple recipe and is full of nutrition. Apples and spinach are a great source of iron and other vitamins. This salad is healthy and delicious. It goes well as a side for many grilled chicken dishes. This is a perfect salad for family and friend get togethers. Once you try this recipe, you will be coming back for more. Go ahead, enjoy your delicious salad.

INGREDIENTS

- 2 ripe apples
- 250 g baby spinach
- 100 g pine nuts
- 1 tsp honey
- 1 tsp lemon juice
- 1 tbsp olive oil

DIRECTIONS

1. Prepare the grill for a medium heat setting.
2. Cut the apples into quarters and remove the seeds. Brush them with olive oil and put them on the grill. Grill for 2 minutes on each side and then set aside.
3. Meanwhile, toast the pine nuts for 2 minutes in a pan and then set aside.
4. In a large salad bowl, tear the baby spinach coarsely. Add to this the apples and the pine nuts.
5. Prepare a salad dressing by whisking together olive oil, honey, and lime juice.
6. Drizzle the dressing on the salad and enjoy your salad.

4.22. Grilled Radicchio Salad

TOTAL TIME
30'

PREPARATION TIME
15'

COOK TIME
15'

SERVING
6

COURSE
SALAD

COUSINE
AMERICAN

This is another popular salad. This salad is popular because of its sweet and tangy dressing. It hits all the correct flavour notes. This salad is a perfect side dish with a lot of grilled recipes. The addition of chopped dill gives it a refreshing flavour. Do try this recipe and you will not be disappointed.

INGREDIENTS

- 1 head romaine lettuce
- 6 green onions
- 1 head red leaf lettuce
- 1 head radicchio
- 3 tbsp olive oil
- 2 tsp chopped dill
- 2 tbsp vinegar
- 2 tsp mustard
- 2 tsp honey
- ¼ tsp salt
- ¼ tsp pepper

DIRECTIONS

1. Prepare the grill for medium heat.
2. Next, prepare the vegetables. Tear the romaine lettuce into four parts, leaving the core connected. Do the same with red leaf lettuce and the radicchio.
3. Brush the lettuce and radicchio with olive oil and season with salt and pepper.
4. Grill the vegetables for 1 minute on each side and take them off from the grill on a large tray.
5. Remove the cores from the vegetables. Cut the radicchio into stripes. Chop the lettuce and chop the green onions.
6. Put in a large salad bowl.
7. In another bowl, make the dressing. Whisk together olive oil, dill, honey, mustard, salt, pepper, and vinegar.
8. Drizzle the dressing on the salad and enjoy your grilled salad.

4.23. Grilled Peach and Arugula Salad

TOTAL TIME
20'

PREPARATION TIME
30'

COOK TIME
10'

SERVING
6

COURSE
SALAD

COUSINE
AMERICAN

In modern times more and more people are using fruits in their salads. This has become a huge trend over the past few years. This recipe is a part of that very trend. Rich in flavour and easy to prepare. This salad can be a perfect choice as a side dish for a huge family get together.

INGREDIENTS

- 2 peaches
- 6 cups fresh arugula
- ½ cup goat cheese
- 3 tbsp apple cider vinegar
- 2 tbsp mustard
- 2 tbsp maple syrup
- 1 small onion finely chopped
- ½ tsp cayenne pepper
- 2 cups long-grain rice
- 2 tbsp olive oil

DIRECTIONS

1. Prepare the grill to get medium heat.
2. Pit the peaches and cut them into quarters.
3. Brush the peaches with olive oil and grill for 2 minutes on each side and set aside.
4. In a large pot, boil water and cook plain rice.
5. Next, make the dressing in a small bowl. Mix the vinegar, shallots, pepper, mustard, oil, and maple syrup. Whisk them together.
6. Now arrange the arugula on a serving plate, top it with rice.
7. Now arrange the grilled peaches on the rice and pour the dressing on it.
8. Top it with crumbled goat cheese.

4.24. Healthy Green SaladSalad

TOTAL TIME
20'

PREPARATION TIME
10'

COOK TIME
10'

SERVING
6

COURSE
SALAD

COUSINE
AMERICAN

As the name suggest this salad is good for your health. Packed with immune boasting components, this salad is perfect for your health. The crunchiness of the romaine lettuce and the soft texture cf avocadoes gives you an amazing food experience. Try this salad and you will not regret it.

INGREDIENTS

- 4 onions
- 2 cups artichoke hearts
- ¼ cup roasted almonds
- 2 tbsp olive oil
- 2 heads of romaine lettuce
- ½ tsp salt
- ½ cup kefir
- ½ avocado
- ½ cup mint leaves
- 2 garlic cloves
- 2 tbsp lemon juice
- ½ cup basil leaves

DIRECTIONS

1. Heat the grill to medium heat. Grill the romaine lettuce heads on the grill with the head side down. Grill for 3 to 5 minutes. Remove the lettuce from the grill and set it aside.
2. Preheat the oven to 425□F and arrange a baking tray with butter paper. Peel and cut the onions into four pieces each and place them on a baking tray. Similarly, cut the artichokes and place them on the same baking tray. Cover the onions and artichoke with olive oil and salt. Toss them and bake for 20 to 30 minutes.
3. Next, in a food processor, add avocado, mint, lemon juice, basil, garlic, and kefir. Puree all the ingredients to make a smooth dressing. Add a bit of water if the dressing is too thick.
4. On a serving platter, arrange the grilled romaine on the base. Remove the cores and arrange the leaves only. Arrange the artichokes and onions on the leaves and drizzle around ½ cup of dressing on top.
5. Enjoy your healthy salad.

4.25. Chili Lime Salad

TOTAL TIME
20'

PREPARATION TIME
5'

COOK TIME
15'

SERVING
8

COURSE
SALAD

COUSINE
AMERICAN

This salad is strictly for someone who can tolerate chilis. This tangy and spicy salad is not for someone who cannot take hot chili flavours. The spices mixed with the tangy flavour of lime make this salad worth trying. If you are someone who would like an experiment with your taste buds, this recipe is just for you.

INGREDIENTS

- 5 corn ears
- 2 roasted piquillo peppers
- ¼ cup cilantro
- ¼ cup crumbled goat cheese
- ¼ tsp salt
- 1 tbsp olive oil
- 2 tbsp lime juice
- ¼ tsp paprika
- ¼ tsp chili powder

DIRECTIONS

1. Heat the grill for a medium heat level.
2. Grill the corn for 4 minutes on each side and take it off from the grill and set it aside to let it rest.
3. Remove the kernels from the corn cobs and put them in a salad bowl.
4. Dice the piquillo pepper and add to the corn. After that, add the cilantro, crumbled cheese, lime juice, salt, paprika, chili powder, and olive oil.
5. Toss everything and enjoy the salad.

4.26. Stuffed Mushrooms

TOTAL TIME
30'

PREPARATION TIME
15'

COOK TIME
15'

SERVING
6

COURSE
SNACK

COUSINE
AMERICAN

This appetizer can even be used as a main course. Generally, it falls in the snack or appetizer category and goes well with most grilled chicken dishes but it is a complete dish on its own as well. Whether you choose to make it as a side dish or a main dish, in both cases you will not regret it. This recipe almost never goes wrong. The steps are easy to follow and the end result is something to look forward to.

INGREDIENTS

- 24 button mushrooms with stems
- ¼ cup parsley
- 1 minced onion
- ¼ cup olive oil
- 2 minced garlic cloves
- ½ cup parmesan cheese
- ½ tsp salt
- ½ cup breadcrumbs
- 1 tsp black pepper

DIRECTIONS

1. Preheat the grill for low to medium heat.
2. In a saucepan heat some olive oil and sauté the onion and minced garlic.
3. In a separate bowl, mix the breadcrumbs, cheese, salt, and black pepper.
4. Next, cut the stems of the mushrooms and chop them into small pieces. Now, add the chopped stems into the saucepan with onions and garlic.
5. Cook for 1 minute.
6. In an aluminum tray set the mushrooms with the heads on the bottom side.
7. Mix the onion and mushrooms with the cheese mixture.
8. Fill the mushroom with one teaspoon of this filling.
9. Put the mushrooms on the grill for 3 to 4 minutes and take them off. Let the mushrooms rest for 2 minutes and then serve them warm.

4.27. Grilled Cauliflower

TOTAL TIME
20'

PREPARATION TIME
10'

COOK TIME
10'

SERVING
3-4

COURSE
SNACK

COUSINE
AMERICAN

This is a simple grilled cauliflower recipe. It goes well with most beef and chicken dishes. However, its combination with seafood does not go well. Take care that not to pair up cauliflower with seafood. Cauliflower is a good addition to your diet as well, cauliflower is a great immunity booster and should be a part of your diet.

INGREDIENTS

- 1 large cauliflower head
- 2 tbsp olive oil
- ¼ tsp chili flakes
- ¼ tsp salt

DIRECTIONS

1. Preheat the grill for low to medium heat.
2. Cut the cauliflowers florets such that a part of stem remains attached to them.
3. Put the cut cauliflower florets in a tray and brush them with olive oil.
4. Season with salt and chili flakes.
5. Grill the cauliflower on the grill for 2 minutes on each side and then put them on a cutting board.
6. Cut the stems and serve the grilled florets.
7. Enjoy your meal.

4.28 Grilled Broccoli

TOTAL TIME
20'

PREPARATION TIME
10'

COOK TIME
10'

SERVING
3-4

COURSE
DISH

COUSINE
AMERICAN

This is another nice side dish. Broccoli goes well with chicken and beef dishes. Easy to make and healthy to eat, you cannot go wrong with broccoli. Broccoli is packed with vitamins and fibre and will be a good choice for you as a side dish. Try out grilling the broccoli and you will not be disappointed.

INGREDIENTS

- 1 large broccoli head
- 2 tbsp olive oil
- ¼ tsp chili flakes
- ¼ tsp salt

DIRECTIONS

1. Preheat the grill for low to medium heat.
2. Cut the broccoli florets such that a part of stem remains attached to them.
3. Put the cut broccoli florets in a tray and brush them with olive oil.
4. Season with salt and chili flakes.
5. Grill the broccoli on the grill for 2 minutes on each side and then put them on a cutting board.
6. Cut the stems and serve the grilled florets.
7. Enjoy your meal.

4.29. Grilled Almonds

TOTAL TIME
20'

PREPARATION TIME
10'

COOK TIME
10'

SERVING
4

COURSE
SNACK

COUSINE
AMERICAN

Almonds are a great source of good fats. This snack is good for your brain health and the good part about it is that you can store it for up to a month. You make one large batch and can enjoy it every day for at least a month.

INGREDIENTS

- 250 g almonds
- 1 tsp olive oil
- ¼ tsp salt
- 20g sesame seeds

DIRECTIONS

1. Heat the grill for medium to high heat.
2. On an aluminum tray, spread the almonds.
3. Brush the almonds with oil and season with salt and sesame seeds.
4. Put the tray on the grill and leave for 10 minutes. Keep tossing the almonds occasionally.
5. Take off the grill and let the almonds rest.
6. The almons can be stored for up to a month.

4.30 Grilled Walnuts

TOTAL TIME
20'

PREPARATION TIME
10'

COOK TIME
10'

SERVING
4

COURSE
SNACK

COUSINE
AMERICAN

This is another healthy snack option. Walnuts are known to have healthy fats which are good for your brain and protect you against neurodegenerative diseases. Walnuts should be a part of your daily diet. This recipe allows you to make a batch that you can store for up to 2 weeks. What are you waiting for? Start preparing your healthy snack.

INGREDIENTS

- 250 g walnuts
- 1 tsp olive oil
- ¼ tsp salt

DIRECTIONS

1. Heat the grill for medium to high heat.
2. On an aluminum tray, spread the walnuts.
3. Brush the walnuts with oil and season with salt.
4. Put the tray on the grill and leave for 10 minutes. Keep tossing the nuts occasionally.
5. Take off the grill and let the nuts rest.
6. The nuts can be stored for up to 2 weeks.

4.31 Grilled Cashew Nuts

TOTAL TIME
20'

PREPARATION TIME
10'

COOK TIME
10'

SERVING
4

COURSE
SNACK

COUSINE
AMERICAN

Nuts are not only delicious; they are healthy as well. Follow this simple recipe to grill cashew nuts. You can make one batch and store them in an air tight container and use it over 2 to 3 weeks. You can even make a mix of different grilled nuts and store it in a container. Make nuts a part of your daily diet because of the many bifacial effects they have on your health.

INGREDIENTS

- 250 g cashew nuts
- 1 tsp olive oil
- ¼ tsp salt

DIRECTIONS

1. Heat the grill for medium to high heat.
2. On an aluminum tray, spread the nuts.
3. Brush the cashew with oil and season with salt.
4. Put the tray on the grill and leave for 10 minutes. Keep tossing the nuts occasionally.
5. Take off the grill and let the nuts rest.
6. The nuts can be stored for up to 2 weeks.

4.32 Grilled Pine Nuts

TOTAL TIME
20'

PREPARATION TIME
10'

COOK TIME
10'

SERVING
4

COURSE
SNACK

COUSINE
AMERICAN

Pine nuts are delicious and packed with energy and nutrition. The grilled pine nuts are easy to prepare and can be stored for up to 3 weeks. You can make one large batch and enjoy your grilled pine nuts every day for the next three weeks.

INGREDIENTS

- 250 g pine nuts
- 1 tsp olive oil
- ¼ tsp salt
- 20 g sesame seeds

DIRECTIONS

1. Heat the grill for medium to high heat.
2. On an aluminum tray, spread the nuts.
3. Brush the pine nuts with oil and season with salt.
4. Put the tray on the grill and leave for 10 minutes. Keep tossing the nuts occasionally.
5. Take off the grill and let the nuts rest.
6. The pine nuts can be stored for up to 3 weeks.

4.33 Grilled Carrot Wedges

TOTAL TIME
20'

PREPARATION TIME
10'

COOK TIME
10'

SERVING
2-3

COURSE
SIDE DISH

COUSINE
AMERICAN

This is a common side dish seen in almost all family get togethers. You can never go wrong with carrots. They are popular among kids and adults alike. Carrots go well with most beef and chicken dishes. So, it is safe to prepare grilled carrots if you are planning to have a big grilling session with friends and family. Apart from being an easy option for a side dish, carrots are a great source of vitamins.

INGREDIENTS

- ½ kg fresh carrots
- 2 tsp olive oil
- ¼ tsp salt

DIRECTIONS

1. Preheat the grill for low to medium heat.
2. Peel the carrots and cut them in wedges.
3. Set them on a tray and brush slightly with olive oil.
4. Season with salt.
5. Next, grill the wedges for 3 minutes on each side.
6. Let the carrots rest for 2 minutes before serving.

4.34 Grilled Potato Wedges

TOTAL TIME
20'

PREPARATION TIME
10'

COOK TIME
10'

SERVING
2-3

COURSE
SIDE DISH

COUSINE
AMERICAN

One of the most favourite food among children and adults alike are potatoes. You can never go wrong with a potato dish. Either they are mashes, boiled, fried or as in this case grilled. Everyone loves to eat potatoes. They go well with almost all chicken, meat and seafood dishes. They are one of the best choice for a side dish.

INGREDIENTS

- ½ kg potatoes
- 2 tsp olive oil
- ¼ tsp salt
- 3 cups water

DIRECTIONS

1. Preheat the grill for low to medium heat.
2. Peel the potatoes and cut them in wedges.
3. In a pot bring water to boil and put the wedges inside. Boil for 5 to 7 minutes then take them out.
4. Set them on a tray and brush slightly with olive oil.
5. Season with salt.
6. Next, grill the wedges for 3 minutes on each side.
7. Let the wedges rest for 2 minutes before serving

4.35 Grilled Sweet Potato

TOTAL TIME
20'

PREPARATION TIME
10'

COOK TIME
10'

SERVING
2-3

COURSE
SIDE DISH

COUSINE
AMERICAN

Sweet potatoes are not as popular among people as the potatoes but still you should try them. You need to develop a certain taste for enjoying sweet potatoes. But once you get a hang of it, you will keep coming back for more.

INGREDIENTS

- ½ kg sweet potatoes
- 2 tsp olive oil
- ¼ tsp salt
- 3 cups water

DIRECTIONS

1. Preheat the grill for low to medium heat.
2. Peel the sweet potatoes and cut them in wedges.
3. In a pot bring water to boil and put the wedges inside. Boil for 5 to 7 minutes then take them out.
4. Set them on a tray and brush slightly with olive oil.
5. Season with salt.
6. Next, grill the wedges for 3 minutes on each side.
7. Let the wedges rest for 2 minutes before serving.

4.36. Grilled Brussel Sprouts

TOTAL TIME
30'

PREPARATION TIME
15'

COOK TIME
15'

SERVING
6

COURSE
SIDE DISH

COUSINE
AMERICAN

Bean sprouts are a great option for a side dish. They can be served with barbecued chicken and are a great source of vitamins and fiber. These are an excellent option for a side dish because they are easy to make and are prepared quickly.

INGREDIENTS

- ½ kg Brussel sprouts
- 3 tbsp olive oil
- 1 tsp salt
- ½ tsp pepper

DIRECTIONS

1. Wash the Brussel sprouts with cold water and dry them out in a colander.
2. Remove the base of the Brussel sprouts and the dried-out parts.
3. In a bowl, mix the olive oil, salt, and pepper.
4. Apply the mixture to the sprouts and put them in a single layer in an aluminum tray.
5. Preheat the grill for low to medium heat.
6. Grill the sprouts for 3 to 4 minutes on each side. Take care that they do not burn.
7. Take them out and serve as a side dish with barbeque chicken.

4.37 Grilled Cherry Tomatoes

TOTAL TIME
10'

PREPARATION TIME
5'

COOK TIME
10'

SERVING
4

COURSE
SIDE DISH

COUSINE
AMERICAN

Grilled cherry tomatoes are not a dish in themselves but can form a base for other dishes like salads and pasta. This recipe is included here because grilled cherry tomatoes add flavor and richness to the foods they are mixed with. To add a rich smoky flavor to pasta, you can add cherry tomatoes. Adding grilled cherry tomatoes to a salad adds the required kick to the otherwise boring salad. Grilled cherry tomatoes are used as a side dish in Middle Eastern food commonly.

INGREDIENTS

- **Cherry Tomatoes 300g**

DIRECTIONS

1. Preheat the grill for low heat.
2. Wash the cherry tomatoes with cold water and spread them on a paper towel.
3. Arrange the cherry tomatoes on the grill and grill on each side for 2 to 3 minutes.
4. Take off from the grill. Serve as a side dish with chicken or put in fresh salads for a rich flavour.

4.38 Apple and Potato Salad

TOTAL TIME
30'

PREPARATION TIME
15'

COOK TIME
15'

SERVING
4-6

COURSE
LUNCH

COUSINE
AMERICAN

This is a simple and easy salad. This is almost like comfort food. The apple and potato salad goes well with most of chicken dishes. It should definitely be part of your next get together. It will be a hit among the kids and adults alike.

INGREDIENTS

- 1 kg apples
- 1 ½ kg potatoes
- 3 tablespoon walnuts
- 3 tablespoon olive oil
- 2 tablespoon mustard sauce
- 1 tablespoon fresh rosemary
- ½ teaspoon black pepper
- Salt to taste.

DIRECTIONS

1. Preheat the grill foe medium to high heat level.
2. Peel and cut the potatoes into 2-inch pieces.
3. Boil 3 cups water in a pot and put the potatoes in it. Let them cook for 5 minutes and then take out. Dry the potatoes on a paper towel.
4. Coat them lightly with olive oil.
5. Top them with salt, pepper, and fresh rosemary.
6. Grill the potatoes for 3 minutes on each side.
7. Take them off the grill and let them rest for 2 minutes till they are firm.
8. Wash the apples and cut them into thick pieces.
9. Brush them lightly with olive oil and grill for two minutes on each side.
10. Toss the apples with the potatoes in a mixing bowl.
11. Make a dressing by combine mustard, lemon juice, and vinegar, and mustard.
12. Drizzle the dressing on the potatoes and apples.
13. Cover the salad and let it cool in the refrigerator.
14. Add some pecans when serving.
15. Sprinkle salt and pepper to finish.

4.39 Grilled Chicken Salad

TOTAL TIME
35'

PREPARATION TIME
15'

COOK TIME
20'

SERVING
2-3

COURSE
SALAD

COUSINE
AMERICAN

This is one of the most delicious salads you will come across. It's a flavourful salad with a tangy and sweet dressing which gives it its distinct flavour. This salad never goes wrong. Once you try this, you will keep coming back for more.

INGREDIENTS

- 250g boneless chicken breasts
- 4 tablespoon vegetable oil
- 1 teaspoon chopped ginger
- 1 teaspoon chopped garlic
- ½ teaspoon pepper
- Salt to taste
- 3 tablespoon lemon juice
- 1 teaspoon honey
- 1 teaspoon dried thyme
- 100g romaine lettuce
- 4 cherry tomatoes
- 1 small onion

DIRECTIONS

1. First, preheat the grill for high heat setting.
2. Put oil, ginger, garlic, salt, and pepper in a mixing bowl. Add chicken to this marinade and thoroughly coat it.
3. Grille the chicken for 7 minutes on each side and take off from the grill. Let the chicken rest before cutting into stripes.
4. Cut cherry tomatoes into halves.
5. Dice the onion thinly.
6. Tear the romaine lettuce and put in a salad bowl.
7. Add the cherry tomatoes and the onions.
8. Take the chicken out and let it cool for 5 minutes.
9. Combine it with other ingredients of the salad.

4.40. Seafood Stuffed Peppers

TOTAL TIME
35'

PREPARATION TIME
20'

COOK TIME
15'

SERVING
4

COURSE
APPETIZER

COUSINE
AMERICAN

This is another appetizer with a mouth-watering flavour. The grilling gives the pepper a nice colour and flavour which makes it an amazing dish to try out. You should definitely try to make this dish and you will not regret.

INGREDIENTS

- 2 green bell peppers
- 12 prawns deveined and chopped
- 1 onion
- 1 Medium Tomato
- 1 tablespoon chopped coriander leaves
- 3 tablespoon cream
- 4 tablespoon grated cheese
- 2 teaspoon lemon juice
- 3 tablespoon olive oil
- ½ teaspoon turmeric powder
- 1 teaspoon red chili
- ¼ teaspoon sugar
- Salt to taste

DIRECTIONS

1. Preheat the grill for low to medium heat setting.
2. Prepare a baking sheet by lining it with butter paper.
3. Cut the bell peppers in half and get rid of the seeds. Clean out the white membranes as well so that a pepper cup is formed.
4. Rub a pinch of salt in each pepper cup.
5. De-vein and wash the prawns. Get rid of the tails. Chop into tiny pieces.
6. Add oil to a frying pan. Stir fry the onions and tomatoes until soft.
7. Add the prawns and al other ingredients except for cream and coriander.
8. Let it fry for 3 to 4 minutes, add the cream and cook on low flame for two minutes.
9. Take off the flame and add coriander.
10. Fill the bell pepper cups with this filling.
11. Top them with cheese.
12. Grill the peppers for 7 minutes on low heat or till the cheese is melted.
13. Serve the delicious bell peppers while they are warm.

4.41. Chicken Stuffed Mushrooms

TOTAL TIME
35'

PREPARATION TIME
20'

COOK TIME
15'

SERVING
8-10

COURSE
APPETIZER

COUSINE
AMERICAN

Another appetizer that is a hot favourite among people. This is an easy recipe, simple to follow and the results are always perfect. This dish can be a part of family dinners or casual get togethers. You should try this recipe and you will not be disappointed.

INGREDIENTS

- 60 mushrooms
- 150g chicken mince
- 2 green onions
- 200g cream cheese
- 2 tablespoon mayonnaise
- 4 tablespoon cheddar cheese
- 2 tablespoon Parmesan cheese
- 2 tablespoon butter
- 2 teaspoon hot sauce
- 1/2 cup breadcrumbs
- Salt to taste
- ½ teaspoon pepper

DIRECTIONS

1. Preheat the grill for medium to high heat setting.
2. Prepare a large baking tray by covering it with aluminum foil.
3. Combine the cream cheese, mayonnaise, and both types of cheese with an electric mixer.
4. Fold the salt, hot sauce, vinegar, onions, and chicken mince into the cheese mixture.
5. Set the mushrooms on the prepared baking tray.
6. Spoon some chicken filling on each mushroom head.
7. On the top of each mushroom, sprinkle some breadcrumbs.
8. Put the mushrooms on the grill for 5 minutes. Take care that the mushrooms don't start burning.
9. Take them off the grill and serve warm.

4.42. Grilled Shrimp

TOTAL TIME
25'

PREPARATION TIME
15'

COOK TIME
10'

SERVING
4-6

COURSE
APPETIZER

COUSINE
AMERICAN

One of the best options for seafood is having a shrimp. Frilled shrimps have this crunchy texture on top with softness of the shrimp meat inside. This is a perfect appetizer to start off any meal. This is the perfect first course.

INGREDIENTS

- 1 kg shrimp peeled and de-veined
- 2 tablespoon lemon juice
- 2 tablespoons chicken stock
- 1 brown onion
- 1/4 cup parsley leaves
- 5 cloves garlic chopped
- 1/3 cup melted butter, divided
- 2 tablespoons parmesan cheese
- ½ cup breadcrumbs
- 1/2 teaspoon crushed red pepper

- flakes
- ½ teaspoon pepper
- Salt to taste
- 2 lemons cut in wedges

DIRECTIONS

1. First of all, preheat the grill for medium heat setting.
2. In a bowl, add the shrimp, chicken stock, ginger, lemon juice, melted butter, pepper, and salt. Mix well.
3. Thread shrimp on skewers and grill them. Grill the shrimps for 3 minutes on each side.
4. Take out the shrimps and assemble in a platter.
5. Mix the leftover melted butter, cheese, breadcrumbs, chili flakes, garlic, and minced parsley in a bowl.
6. Top this shrimp mixture with the breadcrumb mixture.
7. Sprinkle the leftover parsley and lemon juice.
8. Serve while warm.

61

4.43. Potato Cups

TOTAL TIME
55'

This is a delicious recipe but it is not that easy to prepare. You might want to try it three or four times to get perfect results. But this delicious recipe is definitely worth all the hard work and effort.

PREPARATION TIME
20'

INGREDIENTS

- 12 baby potatoes
- 3 green onions chopped
- ¼ cup cream
- 2 tablespoon melted butter
- 2 tablespoon sundried tomatoes chopped
- ¼ teaspoon cayenne pepper
- ½ teaspoon paprika
- ½ teaspoon pepper
- Salt to taste

COOK TIME
35'

SERVING
6-8

DIRECTIONS

1. Preheat the oven to 350°F.
2. Wash and dry the potatoes. Split them lengthwise into two.
3. Melt some butter and grease a baking tray.
4. Put the potatoes face down on the baking tray and bake for 30 minutes.
5. The potatoes should be cooked, and the skin should be intact.
6. Cool the potatoes. Now scoop out the cooked potato leaving the peels in a cup shape. Save this for later use.
7. Mix the potatoes, peas, green onions, sundried tomatoes, cayenne pepper, and melted butter with a hand blender.
8. Add milk and blend till a mashed potato texture is achieved.
9. Fill the potato cups with this filling.
10. Sprinkle some paprika on the filled cups.
11. Now preheat the grill at medium to high heat level.
12. Put the potato cups on the grill and let it grill for 5 to 6 minutes.
13. Take the potato cups off the grill.
14. Serve while warm.

COURSE
APPETIZER

COUSINE
AMERICAN

4.44. Grilled Fish Fingers

TOTAL TIME
45'

PREPARATION TIME
20'

COOK TIME
25'

SERVING
4

COURSE
APPETIZER

COUSINE
AMERICAN

This dish is easy to make and very popular among kids. This is perfect finger food and a great option for an appetizer. Try this recipe out and you cannot go wrong with this one.

INGREDIENTS

- 750g white fish
- 1 egg
- Salt to taste
- 1 teaspoon pepper
- 1 ½ cup breadcrumbs
- 4 tablespoon plain yogurt
- 1 ½ tablespoon chopped dill pickle
- 1 tablespoon dill pickle juice
- 1 tablespoon lemon juice
- 1 teaspoon lemon zest

- 2 teaspoon garlic powder

DIRECTIONS

1. Preheat the grill at medium to high setting.
2. Prepare a baking tray by lining it with aluminum foil.
3. Wash the fish and remove the skin. Cut lengthwise into strips and rub a pinch of salt on each strip.
4. In a deep plate, beat an egg and set it aside.
5. On another deep plate, mix the breadcrumbs, lemon zest, garlic powder, salt, and pepper.
6. Coat each strip with egg and then breadcrumb mixture and set on the baking tray.
7. When all the strips are set on the baking tray, brush each strip with olive oil or oil spray.
8. Next grill the fish fingers on the heated grill. Cook for 4 minutes on each side.
9. Take off the fish fingers form the grill and let them rest.
10. Make tartar sauce by combining the yogurt, dill pickle pieces, dill pickle juice, and lemon juice.
11. Take out fish from the oven and serve with tartar sauce.

4.45. Grilled Prawn Salad

TOTAL TIME
30'

PREPARATION TIME
10'

COOK TIME
2'

SERVING
2

COURSE
APPETIZER

COUSINE
AMERICAN

Another healthy option for women to consume protein is seafood. This is a simple prawn salad recipe that you can take as a snack. The recipe has avocado as well, which serves as an excellent fat source. Avocadoes provide good fat and are extremely beneficial for brain health.

INGREDIENTS

- 1 ripe avocado
- 300 g potatoes
- 250 grams jumbo prawns
- 2 spring onions chopped.
- 1 tbsp Cajun seasoning
- 2 tsp olive oil
- 1 clove garlic minced.
- 1 tsp salt
- 1 cup alfalfa sprouts

DIRECTIONS

1. In a large saucepan, pour water and put in the potatoes. Put in 1 tsp salt and boil the potatoes till cooked.
2. When the potatoes are cooked, let them cool. Then peel and dice into cubes.
3. If you have deveined and peeled prawns, this step can be skipped. Otherwise, peel and devein the prawns. Bring water to boil in a medium-sized pan and put in the prawns. Let them stay for 5 minutes and take them out. Towel-dry the prawns.
4. Preheat the grill for low heat setting.
5. Thread the prawns in skewers and grill them. Grill for 2 minutes on each side. Take them off the grill and then put them in a mixing bowl.
6. In the prawn bowl, add the garlic, spring onion, and Cajun seasoning and mix well.
7. Add the potatoes and toss for 1 to 2 mins.
8. Take the salad out on a salad bowl.
9. Peal and dice an avocado. Top the salad with avocado and alfalfa sprouts.
10. Serve cold.

CHAPTER 5
Grilled Breakfast Recipes

Breakfast is the first and most important meal of the day. It starts your day and sets the tone for the day. It is essential to take a healthy breakfast for a healthy and long life. In this chapter, there are numerous recipes for breakfast that you can prepare on a grill. All the recipes are easy to follow and delicious. When you are finished reading this chapter, you will know what you want for breakfast for the next morning.

5.1. Prosciutto Egg Panini

TOTAL TIME
20'

PREPARATION TIME
10'

COOK TIME
10'

SERVING
8

COURSE
BREAKFAST

COUSINE
AMERICAN

Breakfast is the first meal of the day and it should always be nutritious and full of flavour to wake up all your senses. It is often said that what you have in breakfast sets the tone for the day. This recipe is one that will give your mornings a kick start and light up your day.

INGREDIENTS

- 3 large eggs
- 8 tsp butter
- 2 egg whites
- ½ cup shredded cheddar cheese
- ½ cup milk
- 8 slices prosciutto
- 1 thinly sliced green onion
- 8 slices of sourdough bread
- 1 tbsp mustard
- 1 tbsp maple syrup

- Oil to fry

DIRECTIONS

1. Prepare the eggs by whisking the full eggs with egg whites. Add the green onions. Whisk well. Oil a frying pan and cook the eggs.
2. On four slices of bread, spread the mustard, and on the remaining four, spread the maple syrup. Next, put the eggs on four slices and top with cheddar cheese and prosciutto. Top with the other four slices of bread with maple syrup on the inside.
3. Prepare the grill for medium to high heat setting.
4. Grill the sandwiches for 4 minutes on each side. Take off from the grill and cut the sandwiches diagonally, and serve.

5.2. Sausage and Potato Breakfast

TOTAL TIME
50'

PREPARATION TIME
20'

COOK TIME
30'

SERVING
8

COURSE
BREAKFAST

COUSINE
AMERICAN

Sausages and potatoes are both like warm hugs. They are the perfect comfort food breakfast. This breakfast is ideal for a lazy Sunday morning. Easy to prepare and delicious to eat. Sounds like a perfect breakfast option.

INGREDIENTS

- 1 ½ kg potatoes, cut into cubes
- 300 g sausages cut in ½ inch pieces
- ¼ cup chopped parsley
- ¼ tsp pepper
- 1 chopped onion
- ¼ tsp garlic salt
- ¼ tsp salt

DIRECTIONS

1. Prepare grill for medium heat.
2. In a large bowl, toss the potatoes, sausages, onions, salt, garlic salt, pepper, and parsley.
3. Divide the mixture into eight equal portions.
4. Pack each portion tightly into aluminum foil and put it over the grill for cooking.
5. Leave for 20 minutes and then take off from the grill.
6. Open the packing carefully and let the steam escape.
7. Enjoy your warm breakfast.

5.3. Grilled Honeydew

TOTAL TIME
25'

PREPARATION TIME
15'

COOK TIME
10'

SERVING
6

COURSE
BREAKFAST

COUSINE
AMERICAN

Sometimes you are craving for a little bit of sweetness in the morning. It's always better to get that sweetness from natural sugars rather than rely on artificial flavours. This breakfast option is best for such days. The caramelized sweetness gives it perfect flavour notes. Try out this recipe and you will not be disappointed.

INGREDIENTS

- 1 medium honeydew
- ¼ cup preserved peach
- ¼ tsp grated garlic
- 1 tbsp lemon juice
- 2 tsp lemon zest
- 1 tsp crystallized ginger chopped

DIRECTIONS

1. Prepare the grill for medium heat.
2. Peel and cut the honeydew melon into 2-inch pieces.
3. In a small bowl, mix the peach preserves, lemon zest, garlic, ginger crystals, and lemon juice. Mix well.
4. Thread honeydew on skewers. Now brush half of the glaze on the honeydew pieces.
5. Now grill the honeydew for 4 to 6 minutes with constant turning. Keep replenishing the graze throughout the grilling.
6. Enjoy your breakfast.

5.4. Grilled Fruits with Balsamic Syrup

TOTAL TIME
20'

PREPARATION TIME
10'

COOK TIME
10'

SERVING
4

COURSE
BREAKFAST

COUSINE
AMERICAN

This recipe is easy to prepare and delicious to consume. Fruit sugars are natural and are healthier than the artificial sugars we are used to consuming. The balsamic vinegar gives this recipe a nice tangy touch, this recipe is a must try if you have a sweet tooth. You will not be disappointed.

INGREDIENTS

- 2 plums
- 2 peaches
- 2 nectarines
- 2 tbsp brown sugar
- ½ cup balsamic vinegar

DIRECTIONS

1. In a saucepan, bring balsamic salt and sugar to boil. Keep heating until the liquid is reduced to half.
2. Prepare the grill for low to medium heat.
3. Peel and cut the fruits in half.
4. Grill the fruits for 3 minutes on each side.
5. Set the fruits on a serving plate and tip it with the sweet balsamic sauce.
6. Enjoy your breakfast.

5.5 Grilled Potatoes

TOTAL TIME
40'

PREPARATION TIME
15'

COOK TIME
28'

SERVING
4

COURSE
SIDE DISH

COUSINE
AMERICAN

Potatoes are favourite among people all through the world. This grilled potato recipe never goes wrong. This is a carefully selected and perfected recipe for grilled potatoes. The good thing about potatoes is that they are enjoyed by all age groups alike, either you are a kid or an adult, potato is one thing you will thoroughly enjoy. If you try this recipe you will not at all be disappointed.

INGREDIENTS

- ½ kg baby potatoes
- ½ tsp salt
- ¼ tsp pepper
- 2 tbsp butter
- ½ tsp chopped dill
- ¼ tsp oregano
- ¼ tsp thyme
- ¼ tsp rosemary
- ¼ cup cranberry juice

DIRECTIONS

1. Prepare the grill for medium to high heat settings.
2. Meanwhile, cut the potatoes in halves. Leave the skins on.
3. In a large bowl, add all the ingredients and toss the potatoes in the mixture.
4. Next, pack all potatoes in an aluminum foil and place over the grill for 20 to 30 minutes.
5. After that, take off the grill and carefully open the aluminum foil to release the steam.
6. Serve while warm. Enjoy Your breakfast.

5.6 Grilled Blueberry Bread

TOTAL TIME
50'

PREPARATION TIME
10'

COOK TIME
30'

SERVING
8

COURSE
BREAKFAST

COUSINE
AMERICAN

This is another twist on the famous French toast. This recipe adds the flavour of blueberries which give it a nice flavour profile. The effect of grilling makes this recipe much more aromatic and flavourful. You can almost never go wrong with this recipe. You should try this recipe for a mouth-watering experience.

INGREDIENTS

- 2 cups fresh blueberries
- 1 loaf cinnamon raisin bread
- 2 tbsp maple syrup
- 1 tsp vanilla extract
- ½ cup pecans
- 1 cup cream
- 6 eggs

DIRECTIONS

1. Prepare the grill for medium to high heat setting.
2. In a baking tray, lay an aluminum foil and oil it. Raise its edges and set the bread slices on it.
3. Next, whisk the eggs with vanilla extract, cream, and syrup. Sprinkle with nuts and one cup of blueberry.
4. Pack the aluminum foil and put it over the grill. Cover the grill and let the bread cook for at least 30 minutes.
5. Take off the bread from the grill and carefully open the aluminum foil.
6. Enjoy your bread with the remaining fresh blueberries.

71

5.7 Grilled Burritos

TOTAL TIME
30'

PREPARATION TIME
15'

COOK TIME
15'

SERVING
10

COURSE
BREAKFAST

COUSINE
AMERICAN

Burritos are a famous food option from the Mexican cuisine. Mexican cuisine is famous for its fresh and spicy flavours. This burrito is no exception. This dish is packed with flavour and nutrition value. The recipe includes protein and a variety of fresh vegetables that makes is a healthy food option. If you want to make this even healthier, you can use whole wheat tortillas as well. Try this recipe and you will not regret making it. Who knows it will become a regular part of your diet.

INGREDIENTS

- ½ kg turkey sausage
- 1 tbsp vegetable oil
- 6 cups spinach chopped
- ½ cup feta cheese
- 6 eggs
- 1 cup hash brown potatoes cubed
- 1 red pepper chopped
- 1 onion chopped
- 10 tortillas

DIRECTIONS

1. Preheat the grill for medium heat settings.
2. Beat the eggs in a large bowl.
3. In a frying pan, cook the sausages for 4 to 5 minutes. Then, set aside.
4. In the same pan, heat some oil and add the tomatoes, red pepper, and onions. Cook for 5 to 7 minutes, and then add the spinach. Let it cook for 2 minutes until it is wilted. Add the sausages and eggs. Cook till the eggs are fully cooked.
5. Remove from flame.
6. Spoon the egg filling into each tortilla wrap and top with feta cheese.
7. Fold the burritos and grill for 3 minutes on each side.
8. Enjoy your burritos.

5.8 Breakfast Yummy Skewers

TOTAL TIME
20'

PREPARATION TIME
10'

COOK TIME
10'

SERVING
5

COURSE
BREAKFAST

COUSINE
AMERICAN

This is another interesting breakfast option. This recipe is a sweet and savoury recipe with the goodness of protein, fruit and mushrooms together. This is a heavenly combination. You should try this recipe and you will really enjoy the delicious flavour.

INGREDIENTS

- 200 g cocktail sausages, fully cooked
- 1 tsp Maple syrup
- 10 button mushrooms
- 2 tbsp butter
- 400 g pineapple chunks

DIRECTIONS

1. Prepare the grill for medium to high heat setting.
2. Thread the mushrooms, pineapples, and sausages alternatively to skewers.
3. Grill threaded skewers, around 4 minutes on each side.
4. Enjoy your sausage breakfast.

5.9 Grilled Cheese Panini

TOTAL TIME
15'

PREPARATION TIME
5'

COOK TIME
10'

SERVING
4

COURSE
BREAKFAST

COUSINE
AMERICAN

Grilled cheese is one thing that a lot of people love eating. It is a great example of a comfort food. This recipe gives the good old grilled cheese a flavourful twist. With the addition of herbs to this simple recipe the flavour profile is elevated. Once you try this grilled cheese recipe you will not eat grilled cheese any other way.

INGREDIENTS

- 4 bread slices
- ½ cup cheddar cheese
- ½ cup mozzarella cheese
- ¼ tsp thyme
- ½ tsp oregano

DIRECTIONS

1. Heat the grill for a medium heat setting.
2. On one slice, spread ¼ cup cheddar cheese and ¼ cup mozzarella cheese. Top with a pinch of thyme and oregano. Repeat the same procedure with the second piece of bread as well. Top them both with the remaining pieces of bread.
3. Next, grill the sandwiches for 5 mins on each side.
4. Enjoy your grilled cheese panini.

5.10 Scrambled Egg Panini

TOTAL TIME
35'

PREPARATION TIME
25'

COOK TIME
10'

SERVING
4

COURSE
BREAKFAST

COUSINE
AMERICAN

Sometimes a good sandwich lights up your day. The same can be said about this delicious panini. Made with French bread, you can use any other bread variety of your choice. The flavours are delicious and full of nutrition. Once you try this recipe, you will be coming back for more.

INGREDIENTS

- 1 loaf of French bread
- 6 eggs
- 1 tomato chopped
- 1 cup cubed ham (cooked)
- ¼ tsp pepper
- 1 ½ cup shredded cheddar cheese
- 4 tbsp butter
- 1 chopped onion

DIRECTIONS

1. Prepare the grill for a medium heat setting.
2. Next, prepare the bread loaf. First, cut it diagonally in half in the middle.
3. Then, cut both the pieces lengthwise. Next, hollow each piece and leave till only the crust is left.
4. Cut the pieces of removed bread in cube shape.
5. Spread butter to the insides of the bread crusts.
6. In a pan, add 1 tbsp butter and heat it. Put in chopped onion and cook for 3 to 4 mins and then add the ham and tomato. Cooke for 2 minutes and remove from the flame.
7. In another bowl, whisk eggs and pepper. Heat another pan and melt 2 tbsp butter in it. Pour the egg mixture and scramble it till it is cooked and no liquid remains. Add the ham mixture and cook for 1 more minute.
8. Remove the flame and add 1 cup of cheddar cheese and mix. Add the cubed bread to the mixture and mix well.
9. Spoon this egg filling to the bread crusts and sprinkle with the remaining cheese.
10. Take a large disposable aluminum dish and arrange the bread crusts in it. Cover the container with aluminum foil.
11. Place the aluminum container on the grill and leave for 10 to 12 minutes. Remove the container from the grill and let it rest for 2 minutes before you open the foil. Be careful and let the steam escape.
12. Cut the filled bread into diagonal slices and serve warm.

75

5.11 Grilled Hot Dogs

TOTAL TIME
20'

PREPARATION TIME
10'

COOK TIME
5'

SERVING
6

COURSE
BREAKFAST

COUSINE
AMERICAN

One of the most famous America food. This is a favourite among kids and adults alike. This is the best breakfast opting if you are in a hurry. You can almost never go wrong with hot dogs. Try this recipe and you will not be disappointed.

INGREDIENTS

- 6 pieces sausages
- 6 hot dog burgers
- 4 tbsp mustard
- 2 tbsp butter

DIRECTIONS

1. Prepare the grill for medium to high heat settings.
2. Cut the burgers into half lengthwise and spread butter on the inner sides.
3. Grill the sausages in the grill for 3 minutes on each side.
4. Set aside and then grill the burger buns for 1 minute on each side.
5. Assemble the hot dog and season with mustard.

5.12 Grilled Breakfast Quesadillas

TOTAL TIME
30'

PREPARATION TIME
20'

COOK TIME
10'

SERVING
4

COURSE
BREAKFAST

COUSINE
MEXICAN

This is an amazing recipe and a good healthy breakfast option. If you want to make this healthier, try it with whole wheat tortillas. This recipe can also be made with gluten free tortillas if you have any food restrictions. The eggs in the recipe gives you a perfect punch of morning protein boost. The grilled flavour is a mouth-watering experience. You should definitely try this recipe and you will not regret it.

INGREDIENTS

- 2 tbsp unsalted butter
- 4 tortillas
- ½ diced bell pepper
- 2 tbsp milk
- 1 tbsp green onion
- 4 eggs
- ¼ diced onion
- 200 g cheddar cheese
- 200 g mozzarella cheese

DIRECTIONS

1. Preheat the grill to medium to high heat setting.
2. Add 1 tbsp butter to the frying pan and let it melt. Add onion and bell pepper and let it cook for 5 minutes with constant stirring.
3. Please take out the vegetables and set them aside.
4. In the same frying pan, add more butter and put it back on the flame. Whisk the eggs and put them in the heated pan. Stir while cooking, and then add the onion and bell peppers to the eggs. Stir and m x well. Remove from the flame.
5. Now prepare the tortillas. On half of the tortilla, put a hand full of cheddar cheese and then mozzarella cheese. Now, put a layer of cooked egg and ham mix and top it again with both varieties of cheese.
6. Close the tortilla bread and grill on both sides for 4 minutes each. Take care not to burn the tortilla.
7. Please take off the tortilla from the grill and let it rest for two minutes before cutting it into pieces.
8. Enjoy your breakfast quesadillas.

5.13 Peach and Burrata Crostini

TOTAL TIME
25'

PREPARATION TIME
10'

COOK TIME
15'

SERVING
12

COURSE
BREAKFAST

COUSINE
AMERICAN

This is a great recipe for a savoury breakfast. Try out this delicious recipe and you will not regret. This recipe is not like your conventional breakfast but is much more. It gives you great flavour notes and a new experience. Do try this recipe and you will be in for a treat.

INGREDIENTS

- 1 loaf French bread cut into ½ inch pieces
- 4 tbsp olive oil
- 4 sliced peaches
- 2 tbsp balsamic vinegar
- 2 balls burrata cheese
- 1 bunch basil leaves
- 150 g sliced prosciutto
- ¼ tsp salt
- ¼ tsp pepper

DIRECTIONS

1. Preheat the grill to medium to high heat.
2. Brush the peach slices and baguette with olive oil, and then season with salt and pepper.
3. Grill the peaches, 2 minutes on each side. Take care that they do not become soft. Otherwise, it will be difficult to pick up from the grill.
4. Next, grill the baguette on both sides for 2 minutes each and take off from the grill.
5. Next, you plate the ingredients properly. Put the crostini and put some basil leaves on the top, then add one tbsp of burrata. Then, on top of it, put a slice of peach and put a slice of prosciutto in the end. In the top, drizzle some vinegar.
6. Enjoy your food.

5.14 Grilled Pita Pizza

TOTAL TIME
30'

PREPARATION TIME
10'

COOK TIME
25'

SERVING
2

COURSE
BREAKFAST

COUSINE
AMERICAN

Who does not love pizza? Pizza is one of the most popular foods among the population. Tis pizza is a bit different, in this pizza we have used pita in place of pizza crust. This little twist makes this dish more interesting and worth trying.

INGREDIENTS

- 1 cup sliced button mushrooms
- 2 large eggs
- 4 tbsp olive oil
- 2 tbsp parmesan cheese
- 2 garlic cloves minced
- 1 cup arugula
- 4 slices of prosciutto
- ½ cup mozzarella cheese
- 2 wheat pitas
- ½ cup marinara sauce

- ¼ tsp salt

DIRECTIONS

1. Preheat the oven at 375°F.
2. Wash the mushrooms well and pat them dry. Heat 2 tbsp oil in a frying pan. Add the mushrooms and minced garlic, and salt. Sauté for 5 minutes and then remove from heat and set aside.
3. Preheat the grill to medium heat. Brush olive oil on both sides of both the wheat pitas and grill them. Grill the pita for 3 minutes on each side.
4. Meanwhile, tear the prosciutto into 2-inch pieces.
5. Prepare a large baking sheet with butter paper. Put the pitas on the baking sheets. Spread the marinara sauce equally on both the pits. Next, top with the mozzarella cheese. Next, top with the prosciutto and mushrooms. Bake the pitas for 10 minutes.
6. When the pitas are out, set them aside.
7. In a frying pan, add 2 tbsp olive oil and fry two eggs with a sunny side up. Top the pizzas with these eggs. Sprinkle with parmesan cheese.
8. Serve warm and enjoy your breakfast.

5.15 Grilled Grapefruit

TOTAL TIME
10'

PREPARATION TIME
5'

COOK TIME
5'

SERVING
1

COURSE
BREAKFAST

COUSINE
AMERICAN

This recipe is highly recommended. You should try this recipe. Not only is it delicious, it has high nutritional value. Grape fruit is an amazing anti-oxidant and is great to detoxify your blood. This recipe has honey as well. Honey itself has antiseptic qualities. This recipe is one you make for yourself every week. If you love yourself you will definitely try this recipe.

INGREDIENTS

- 1 grapefruit
- 2 tbsp yogurt
- 1 tbsp honey
- 1 tsp brown sugar

DIRECTIONS

1. Preheat the grill for low to medium heat.
2. Cut the grapefruit in half. On the flesh side of the fruit, rub sugar on both sides.
3. Grill the grapefruits for 5 minutes with flesh side down.
4. Take off from the grill and let it rest.
5. Mix the honey and yogurt.
6. On a plate, put the grapefruit and serve with the honey yogurt on the side.

5.16 Grilled Banana with Chocolate

TOTAL TIME
20'

PREPARATION TIME
10'

COOK TIME
10'

SERVING
2-3

COURSE
BREAKFAST

COUSINE
AMERICAN

Sometimes we crave for something sweet for breakfast. This is a perfect option for such days. This is an ultimate treat for breakfast. Children and adults will enjoy this recipe alike.

INGREDIENTS

- 3 bananas
- 2 tbsp brown sugar
- ¼ cup cream cheese
- 2 tbsp icing sugar
- 2 tbsp butter
- 20 g cooking chocolate

DIRECTIONS

1. Preheat the grill for low to medium heat
2. Peel the bananas and cut them in half lengthwise.
3. Melt butter and brush it on the banana lightly.
4. Grill the bananas for one minute on each side and set them on a platter.
5. In a frying pan, melt butter and add brown sugar. Let the sugar cook with butter and wait for it to caramelize lightly. When the sugar starts to caramelize, stop the flame. Brush this glaze on the bananas.
6. In a small cup, put the cooking chocolate and melt it in the microwave.
7. Drizzle the melted chocolate on the bananas.
8. In another bowl, whisk together cream cheese and icing sugar. Fill the mixture in a piping bag and pipe some flowers on the serving plate.
9. Enjoy your breakfast.

5.17 Eggs Benedict Burger

TOTAL TIME
35'

PREPARATION TIME
20'

COOK TIME
15'

SERVING
3

COURSE
BREAKFAST

COUSINE
AMERICAN

This is one of the most famous American breakfast. This recipe will give you the real flavour of America's food and breakfast culture. You should try this recipe for its taste as well as its nutritional value.

INGREDIENTS

- 3 eggs
- ¼ tsp pepper
- 1 tbsp water
- ¼ tsp salt
- 100 g butter cut into cubes
- 2 tsp lemon juice
- ½ kg minced beef
- 3 burger buns
- 2 tsp Worcestershire sauce
- 3 slices of bacon

- 3 poached eggs

DIRECTIONS

1. Preheat the grill for medium to high heat setting.
2. Heat water in a water bath. Place a pot or bowl over the water bath and whisk 3 egg yolks on the bowl. Add 1 tbsp of water. Keep whisking thoroughly till the mixture thickens.
3. Remove from heat and then add lemon juice and mix it.
4. Add 1 tsp of butter and whisk in the egg mixture. Season with salt and pepper. This is the hollandaise sauce.
5. Next, in a large mixing bowl, season the beef with Worcestershire sauce, salt, and pepper. Mix well. Prepare 3 large patties with the ground beef.
6. Grill the patties of 4 minutes on each side and let them rest.
7. Grill the burger buns on both sides for one minute each.
8. Now assemble the burgers. On the bun, put the patty, then the bacon strip, the poached egg, and then top with the hollandaise sauce.
9. Serve warm.

5.18 Grilled Asparagus with Poached Egg

TOTAL TIME
30'

PREPARATION TIME
15'

COOK TIME
15'

SERVING
4

COURSE
BREAKFAST

COUSINE
AMERICAN

This is an amazing recipe packed with nutrition. It is loaded with iron, protein and vitamins. Asparagus should be a part of your diet. It is a rich source of protein and fibre. Both these components are essential for your health and wellbeing. Apart from being nutritious, this recipe is delicious. You can start your day with this mouth-watering grilled asparagus recipe.

INGREDIENTS

- 4 eggs
- 4 tbsp pesto sauce
- 2 tbsp vinegar
- ¼ cup parmesan cheese
- 1 iced bowl water
- 8 slices baguette
- 16 pieces asparagus
- 8 slices of ham
- 2 tbsp olive oil

DIRECTIONS

1. Poach the four eggs.
2. Preheat the grill to medium heat.
3. Brush the asparagus with olive oil and season with salt. Grill the asparagus for 3 to 5 minutes.
4. Assemble the dish. First, plate the toasted baguette and put a slice of ham on it. Now arrange the asparagus on the plate and place the poached egg on the grilled asparagus.
5. Drizzle with pesto sauce and top with parmesan cheese.
6. Enjoy your delicious food.

5.19 Grilled French Toast

TOTAL TIME
30'

PREPARATION TIME
15'

COOK TIME
15'

SERVING
5

COURSE
BREAKFAST

COUSINE
FRENCH

This is a nice twist on the popular French toast. The flavour of grilled French toast gives a new dimension to this recipe. The taste is delicious and mouth-watering. You should try this recipe and you will not be disappointed.

INGREDIENTS

- 5 slices of sourdough bread
- ¼ tsp salt
- 1 tsp coconut oil
- 1 ½ tsp almond milk
- ¼ tsp cinnamon
- ¼ cup orange zest
- ¼ tsp vanilla
- 150 g silk tofu
- 1 tsp maple syrup
- 1 banana

- 1 tbsp peanut butter

DIRECTIONS

1. Warm up the peanut butter and mix it with maple syrup.
2. Put all the liquid ingredients in a blender and blend well. Then pour into a shallow casserole dish.
3. Preheat the grill for medium heat.
4. Dip the bread slices in the liquid mixture and grill on each side for 3 minutes.
5. Plate on a large dish and garnish with orange zest, cinnamon, and sliced banana.
6. Serve the peanut butter and maple sauce at the side.
7. Enjoy your French toast.

5.20 Grilled Sausage with Eggs and Kale

TOTAL TIME
30'

PREPARATION TIME
10'

COOK TIME
20'

SERVING
2-3

COURSE
BREAKFAST

COUSINE
AMERICAN

This is a nice twist to the conventional sausages. The egg and kale give this dish a nutritious profile. This breakfast can be a perfect way to start off your day. This recipe can easily be used for family get together and brunches as well.

INGREDIENTS

- 2 cups kale
- 4 eggs
- 1 medium yellow onion
- 4 large sausages
- 2 tbsp olive oil
- 1 cup button mushroom sliced

DIRECTIONS

1. Preheat the grill for medium to high heat settings.
2. Chop the two cups of kale.
3. In a frying pan, add oil and sliced onions and mushrooms. Sauté for three minutes and add the kale.
4. When the kale becomes a bright green, then break the four eggs in the frying pan. Take off from the heat and place the pan on the grill. The frying pan should be made of cast iron.
5. Grill the sausages by grilling them for 3 to 4 minutes on each side. Take off the sausages.
6. Set the sausages on the sides of the pans.
7. Enjoy your breakfast.

5.21 Grilled Avocado Toast

TOTAL TIME
15'

PREPARATION TIME
10'

COOK TIME
5'

SERVING
1-2

COURSE
BREAKFAST

COUSINE
AMERICAN

This is an easy and quick recipe that is packed with protein and healthy fat. It gives you an energy boost. It is best to use ripe avocadoes for this recipe. Underdone avocadoes may taste bitter and bland.

INGREDIENTS

- 1 egg
- 1 ripe avocado
- 1 small onion is finely chopped.
- 2 brown bread slices
- ½ tsp salt
- ½ tsp black pepper

DIRECTIONS

1. Hard boil the egg.
2. Mash the avocado pulp in a medium-sized bowl.
3. Mix the salt, pepper, and onion.
4. When the egg is hard-boiled, peel it and mash it. Add it to the avocado mixture.
5. Make the mixture smooth.
6. Heat the grill for medium heat setting.
7. Brush the bread slices with olive oil.
8. Spread one side of the bread slice with avocado filling. Top it with the other bread slice.
9. Put the sandwich on the grill and heat for 3 minutes on each side.
10. Take off the sandwich and cut it diagonally. Serve while still warm and toasty.

5.22 Grilled Chicken and Egg Wraps

TOTAL TIME
30'

PREPARATION TIME
15'

COOK TIME
15'

SERVING
2

COURSE
BREAKFAST

COUSINE
MEXICAN

This is a delicious recipe that is rich in protein. This is a simple recipe that can be made in under 20 minutes. The grilling gives the simple wrap a nice toasty and crisp effect. You should try this recipe and you will not regret it.

INGREDIENTS

- 3 large eggs
- 1 chicken fillet cut into small cubes.
- 1 tsp salt
- 1 tsp pepper
- 1 tsp minced garlic
- 1 small onion chopped.
- 1 small tomato chopped.
- 2 whole-wheat wraps
- ¼ cup olive oil

DIRECTIONS

1. In a frying pan, put 2 tbsp olive oil and crackle garlic in the pan.
2. Add the onions and cook for 2 minutes. Then add the chicken, salt, and pepper.
3. Cook for 4 to 5 mins.
4. Add the tomatoes and cook for further 5 minutes on medium flame.
5. Take off the chicken from the stove.
6. Next, whisk the eggs and scramble them in a frying pan.
7. Next, put both the fillings in the wraps and fold them.
8. Turn on the grill at medium heat and grill the filled wraps on the grill.
9. Grill the wrap for 2 minutes on each side.
10. Serve warm.

5.23 Grilled Vanilla French Toast

TOTAL TIME
1H 30'

PREPARATION TIME
40'

COOK TIME
10'

SERVING
2

COURSE
BREAKFAST

COUSINE
FRENCH

This is a nice twist on the popular French toast. The flavour of vanilla gives a new dimension to the French toast recipe. The taste is delicious and mouth-watering. You should try this recipe and you will not be disappointed.

INGREDIENTS

- 2/3 a cup of milk
- 1 tsp of ground cinnamon
- 1/2 cup of sugar
- 4 eggs
- 1/2 tsp of table salt
- 2 tsp vanilla essence (or a scraped vanilla bean)
- 1 white bread loaf
- ½ cup of milk

DIRECTIONS

1. Cut white bread loaf into thick slices. The slices should be thick enough to soak in the custard.
2. Mix the milk, sugar, cream, salt, vanilla essence, and ground cinnamon.
3. Whisk well to form a smooth custard-like batter.
4. Arrange a rimmed dish with bread slices. On the slices, pour custard.
5. Let the custard soak for 25 minutes, then flip the slices after 10 minutes to ensure soaking evenly. Be sure that the custard soaks to the center as well as the corners of the slices.
6. You might even let the entire tray soak in the refrigerator overnight.
7. Now, line a baking dish with butter paper. Shift the soaked slices to the prepared baking dish, arranging that there is a little gap between the slices.
8. Preheat the grill. Put the baking dish on the grill and cover the grill or if the grill cannot be covered, cover the baking dish with aluminum sheet.
9. After 30 minutes, check the dish. The slices should be soft but be sure that they are not soggy. If they are still wet, grill for another 5 minutes.
10. Serve with fresh fruits.
11. Serve warm.

CHAPTER 6
Grilled Main Course Recipes

For a cook or chef, this is the most important course. If you wish to become a good cook, you have to have some signature main course dishes. Even if you are a family cook, some specialty dishes may set you apart even among the family. This chapter will find many recipes that you can choose from to practice and perfect over time. There are recipes for everyone. If you are a meat lover, you have a lot of choices topic up from. If you love some seafood, there are tons of seafood recipes. If you are strictly vegetarian, there are a couple of recipes for you as well. No matter who you are and what you like, there is a special recipe for you somewhere in these carefully selected recipes. The recipes follow a simple approach and clear instructions so that it is easy for everyone to follow.

6.1. Grilled Salmon

TOTAL TIME
20'

PREPARATION TIME
10'

COOK TIME
10'

SERVING
3

COURSE
LUNCH

COUSINE
AMERICAN

The best thing about this recipe is that it is easy to make and quick to prepare. Minimum ingredients are used to achieve perfection with this smoked salmon. Try this recipe, and you will be in for a mouth-watering treat.

INGREDIENTS

- 1 kg fresh Salmon
- 2 tbsp brown sugar
- 1 tsp dried dill
- 1 tsp pepper
- 1 tsp salt

DIRECTIONS

1. Wash and pat dry the fish carefully. You must be careful with raw fish meat because it is delicate and can break.
2. Mix the salt, pepper, sugar, and dill in a bowl.
3. Rub this sugar mixture on the top side of the fish.
4. Put it in the refrigerator for one hour. This will allow the fish to dry brine.
5. Preheat the grill for medium to high heat.
6. Take out the fish and let it come to room temperature.
7. Grill the fish for 4-5 mins on each side.
8. The dish can be served at room temperature or even cold.

6.2. Spicy Grilled Chicken

TOTAL TIME
1 HOUR

PREPARATION TIME
30'

COOK TIME
3'

SERVING
4

COURSE
DINNER

COUSINE
AMERICAN BBQ

Chicken is one of the most widely popular food throughout the world. This recipe gives the grilled chicken a spicy and flavourful twist. The brown sugar used in the rub gives it a caramelized look and texture and adds richness to the taste. Try this recipe out, and you will not be disappointed.

INGREDIENTS

- 1 medium-sized whole chicken with skin
- 1 tbsp thyme
- 2 tbsp cayenne pepper
- 1 tbsp garlic powder
- 2 tbsp chili powder
- 1 tbsp salt
- 2 tbsp sugar
- 1 tbsp onion powder
- 2 tbsp black pepper
- 3 tbsp olive oil

DIRECTIONS

1. Preheat the grill for medium to high heat setting.
2. In a medium-sized mixing bowl, mix the thyme, cayenne pepper, garlic powder, chili powder, salt, sugar, onion powder, and black pepper. This will make the perfect rub for the chicken.
3. First, rub the whole chicken with olive oil. All sides and inside the hollow cavity of chicken as well.
4. After that, apply the prepared rub on the chicken generously. Rub it on the entire surface of the chicken.
5. Put the skin over the breast of the chicken and apply the rub under the skin as well.
6. Cut the chicken into 8 pieces with a butcher's knife.
7. Grill the chicken pieces for 7 minutes on each side.
8. Served the grilled chicken warm.

91

6.3. Grilled Corn on the Cob

TOTAL TIME
4H 30'

PREPARATION TIME
4 HOURS

COOK TIME
30'

SERVING
6

COURSE
LUNCH

COUSINE
AMERICAN

Corn on the cob is a crowd's favourite side dish. It is popular among kids and adults alike. These complement all sorts of meats in a barbecue and give us that much-needed light and sweet flavours in the middle of a high protein barbecue. Try this easy recipe, and you will not regret preparing some smoked corn on the cob.

INGREDIENTS

- 6 pieces ear corn with husks
- Brown sugar 2 tbsp
- Salt ½ tsp
- Garlic powder ½ tsp
- Melted butter ¼ cup.
- Onion powder 1 tsp
- Sliced green onion 3 pieces.

DIRECTIONS

1. Take a large roasting pot and fill it half with room temperature water.
2. Pull the husks of all the corn cobs and remove the silks. Let the husks remain attached to the cob but just pulled back.
3. Soak the corn cobs in the water and if needed, fill the pot with more water to completely immerse the cobs into water.
4. Soak for 4 hours.
5. After that, remove the cobs from the pot, place them on paper towels, and let them dry.
6. Preheat the grill for medium to high heat setting.
7. In a mixing bowl, mix the butter, sugar, salt, onion powder, and garlic powder to make a rub for the corn on the cob.
8. With the help of a brush, apply the rub generously to the corn cobs
9. Grill the corn cobs for 5 to 6 minutes on each side.
10. Let them rest for 10 minutes, and then serve them as a delicious side dish.

92

6.4. Grilled Chicken with Asparagus

TOTAL TIME
5 HOURS

PREPARATION TIME
3 HOURS

COOK TIME
2 HOURS

SERVING
3

COURSE
LUNCH

COUSINE
AMERICAN

This delicious chicken recipe is perfect for enjoying on the weekend. It is easy to make and takes a short while to prepare. The juicy chicken with the light smokiness is a success with kids and adults alike. This dish will be a crowd favorite. Try out this recipe and enjoy it with friends and family.

INGREDIENTS

For Chicken:
- 3 to 4 pieces chicken thighs
- 5 tbsp store-bought BBQ rub
- water as required.
- 1 tsp sugar
- 1 tsp salt
- ¼ cup apple cider vinegar

For Asparagus
- 1 bunch asparagus
- 1 tsp red pepper flakes
- ¼ cup balsamic vinegar
- 1 tsp pepper
- 1 tsp salt

DIRECTIONS

1. Prepare to brine the chicken thighs. Put the chicken in a large zip lock bag, then add Vinegar, salt, and sugar.
2. Then, fill the bag with water such that the chicken pieces are completely soaked. Put it in the refrigerator for 2 to 3 hours.
3. The brining process will ensure that the chicken does not dry out while grilling.
4. Similarly, prepare a marinade for the asparagus bunch as well. Please put it in a large zip lock bag. Add the balsamic vinegar, salt pepper, pepper flakes, and water to soak the asparagus. Please leave it in the refrigerator for 3 hours.
5. Prepare a small BBQ spray bottle having one part vinegar, two parts water, and 1 tsp sugar. Mix it properly. This will be used to spray on the chicken while it is being grilled
6. Take the chicken out of the refrigerator after 2 hours and wash and dry the pieces.
7. Apply the BBQ rub generously on the chicken pieces.
8. Preheat the grill for medium to high heat.
9. Place the chicken on the grill. Grill for at least 10 minutes on each side with flipping occasionally. Spray with the BBQ spray bottle after every 2 to 3 minutes. This will prevent the chicken from drying.
10. Grill for about 15 to 20 mins.
11. Take the chicken off and let it rest for 5 minutes.
12. Meanwhile, please take out the asparagus and spread it on a paper towel, and pat dry.
13. Put the asparagus on the grill. Grill for 2 minutes on each side and then take off from the grill.
14. Serve the chicken with a side of asparagus.
15. This is a good pairing to serve, and the asparagus complements the grilled chicken beautifully.

6.5. Grilled Turkey Breast

TOTAL TIME
50'

PREPARATION TIME
25'

COOK TIME
25'

SERVING
3-4

COURSE
LUNCH

COUSINE
AMERICAN

Turkey has often been bland and boring meat. This recipe gives the turkey a tasty and spicy twist. The BBQ sauce mixed with hot sauce and honey gives the grilled turkey a rich flavor and an amazing texture. Try out this mouth-watering and delicious recipe and enjoy the aromatic and tender turkey meat. This recipe never disappoints.

INGREDIENTS

- 1 piece turkey breast 1 piece
- 4 tbsp store-bought BBQ rub
- 3 tbsp olive oil
- 100 g butter
- 2 tsp hot Tabasco sauce
- 1 tsp honey

DIRECTIONS

1. First, preheat the grill for medium to high heat.
2. Next, prepare the turkey meat. Cover the whole meat with a layer of olive oil. Rub the oil generously.
3. Then apply the BBQ rub on the whole meat piece. Rub the mixture generously so that the whole turkey breast is covered with the BBQ rub.
4. In a heatproof cup, prepare the basting mixture for the turkey. Add the butter, cut into small cubes to the cup. Put in the honey, hot sauce, and ¼ teaspoon BBQ rub.
5. Put the turkey and basting mixture on the grill. Let the turkey breast cook for 10 to 15 minutes on each side while flipping occasionally.
6. After a while, you will see that the basting mixture is steaming.
7. Pour the basting mixture about 2 tbsp on the meat and let it smoke.
8. Repeat the procedure with the basting mixture after every 2 to 3 minutes.
9. Take off the meat from the grill when it becomes tender.
10. Let the meat rest for 15 minutes, and then slice it.
11. Serve this mouth-watering and delicious meal to your friends and family.

6.6. Grilled Potatoes

TOTAL TIME
1 HOUR

PREPARATION TIME
10'

COOK TIME
50'

SERVING
4

COURSE
SIDE DISH

COUSINE
AMERICAN

Baked potatoes are an all-time favorite side dish. They go well with all meats, especially chicken. They can be served as it is or with a rich sour cream. This is an easy and useful recipe to smoke potatoes perfectly. This recipe is simple and easy to prepare and goes well with almost anything. You can even make this and have it on its own. It is great comfort food. Try it out, and you will not be disappointed.

INGREDIENTS

- 4 medium-sized potatoes
- ¼ cup Olive oil
- 1 tsp granular Salt

DIRECTIONS

1. Preheat the grill for a high heat setting.
2. Wash the potatoes and dry them on a paper towel.
3. Poke each potato with a fork 5 or six times at different places on the potato surface. This will prevent the potato from exploding when it is exposed to a high temperature.
4. Brush the potatoes generously with olive oil.
5. Season the potatoes with salt.
6. Place the potatoes near the charcoal in the grill.
7. After 45 minutes, check the potatoes for doneness.
8. When the potatoes are being cooked, you can use the grill and crate to grill other things.
9. Take the potatoes out and let them rest for 10 minutes.
10. Slit the potatoes from the entrance and fill them with American-style chili if you want to serve as a main dish.
11. Another serving idea is to slit the center and fill it with sour cream and top it with sliced green onions. This makes a perfect side dish.

6.7. Grilled Burgers

TOTAL TIME
30'

PREPARATION TIME
10'

COOK TIME
20'

SERVING
6

COURSE
LUNCH

COUSINE
AMERICAN

Burgers are a staple food in American cuisine. These smoked beef burgers have a smoky flavor and are perfect for a quiet weekend lunch with the family. The burgers do not have a sauce but are still delicious and mouth-watering. The best part about this recipe is that it is easy to make, and it takes less time for preparation and cooking. Try this recipe and enjoy it with friends and family.

INGREDIENTS

- 6 pieces pre-prepared beef burger patties
- Salt 2 tbsp
- Garlic Powder ½ tbsp
- Pepper 1 tbsp
- Dehydrated onion ½ tbsp

DIRECTIONS

1. Make sure that the burger patties are at room temperature.
2. Preheat the grill at a high-temperature setting.
3. In a mixing bowl, add the salt, pepper, garlic powder, and dehydrated onion. Mix these ingredients well such that a rub is formed.
4. Apply this rub on the burger patties. Cover both sides of the burger patty with the rub.
5. Grill the burger patties for 8 minutes on eat side and then set them aside for assembly.
6. Next, prepare the buns by putting them on a grill. Grill the buns for one minute on each side and then assemble.
7. Assemble the burgers with fresh vegetables like onion, lettuce, and tomatoes.
8. Serve warm.

6.8. Grilled Drum Sticks

TOTAL TIME
3 HOURS

PREPARATION TIME
15'

COOK TIME
2H 30'

SERVING
6

COURSE
DINNER

COUSINE
AMERICAN

This is a recipe for mouth-watering and flavourful drumsticks. The flavors are sweet and spicy. This recipe is prepared in 2 ½ hours, and you can enjoy these tasty drumsticks with BBQ sauce. Do try this recipe; this is a hit among kids and adults alike.

INGREDIENTS

- 1 ½ kg chicken drumsticks
- ½ cup store-bought steak rub
- 1 tsp cayenne pepper
- ½ cup BBQ sauce
- 5 tbsp Tabasco sauce

DIRECTIONS

1. Wash and pat dry the drumsticks.
2. Do not remove the skins from the chicken drumsticks.
3. Rub the drumsticks with the store-bought steak rub and the cayenne pepper. Keep the drumsticks in the refrigerator for 2 hours.
4. Preheat the grill for medium to high heat setting.
5. Please take out the drumsticks from the refrigerator and wait for 15 minutes before grilling them.
6. Grill the drumstick by grilling them for seven minutes on each side. Take the drumsticks off the grill and onto a plate.
7. Let the drumsticks rest for 3 to 4 minutes.
8. Meanwhile, mix the BBQ sauce and tabasco sauce in a bowl.
9. Dip all the drumsticks in the sauce one by one and arrange them on a platter.
10. Serve these delicious drumsticks to your friends and family.

6.9. Grilled Mac and Cheese

TOTAL TIME
2H 30'

PREPARATION TIME
30'

COOK TIME
2 HOURS

SERVING
4

COURSE
SIDE DISH

COUSINE
AMERICAN

Mac and cheese as comfortable as comfort foods get. It serves as a great side dish with your barbeque. It is conventionally made in an oven, but you can also use a smoker to prepare this dish to give an extra smoky richness.

INGREDIENTS

- ½ kg Elbow Macaroni
- 3 cups milk
- ¼ cup flour
- 500 g grated cheese
- 250 g Cream cheese
- ¼ cup butter
- Salt to taste
- Pepper to taste

DIRECTIONS

1. First, boil 12 cups of water in a medium cooking pot. When the water comes to a boil, add the elbow macaroni, and let it boil for 8 to 10 minutes. When the macaroni is boiled, remove all the water, and put the macaroni aside.
2. Next, you will prepare the cheese sauce.
3. In a medium-sized pan, put in the butter in melt it over the flame. After the butter is melted, add the flour, and mix it. Cook for about two minutes till the flour starts to brown.
4. Next, add the milk and cook for five minutes with constant stirring or whisking to not form lumps. Let the milk thicken. When the milk starts to thicken, take the saucepan off the flame, and add cream cheese.
5. Mix the cream cheese and make a smooth mixture.
6. In a heat-resistant bowl, add the cheese. Pour this mixture over the cheese and mix well.
7. Now turn on the grill at medium heat level.
8. Now take an aluminum tray and spread the cooked macaroni in its base.
9. Pour the cream and cheese mixture over the macaroni such that it is fully immersed in the mixture.
10. Put the aluminum tray on the grill and close the hood.
11. Let it stay for 1 hour and then take out. Let it rest for a few minutes.
12. Enjoy your mac and cheese separately or with barbequed chicken or meat.

6.10. Grilled Ribs

TOTAL TIME
4H 30'

PREPARATION TIME
30'

COOK TIME
4 HOURS

SERVING
4

COURSE
DINNER

COUSINE
AMERICAN

If you are someone who enjoys the ribs on the bone, this recipe is just for you. You will enjoy the rich smokiness of the ribs flavoured with mild herbs served with BBQ sauce. Preparing BBQ ribs might be a bit tricky if you go the conventional way, but the ribs prepared in the electric Smoker save you all the hassle, giving you the same flavor.

INGREDIENTS

- 1 ½ kg one cut of ribs
- 1 tsp black pepper
- 1 tsp paprika
- 2 tsp garlic powder
- ¼ cup brown sugar
- 1 tsp salt
- ¼ cup BBQ sauce

DIRECTIONS

1. Prepare the ribs. Trim the extra fat and cut the ribs.
2. Next, prepare the rub for the ribs. In a bowl, mix the pepper, paprika, salt, garlic powder, brown sugar, and salt.
3. Rub this mixture on the ribs generously such that all parts of the ribs are rubbed with the herbs.
4. Put the ribs in a large zip lock bag and put them in the refrigerator overnight.
5. The next day, preheat the grill.
6. Bring out the ribs from the fridge and wait for them to get to room temperature.
7. Place the ribs on the grill and close the grill hood.
8. After 20 minutes, open the hood and turn the ribs and close the hood again.
9. Let the ribs grill for 20 more minutes.
10. Take the ribs out and let them rest for 5 minutes.
11. After that, enjoy the delicious ribs.

6.11. Grilled Beef Jerky

TOTAL TIME
5 HOURS

PREPARATION TIME
30'

COOK TIME
3 HOURS

SERVING
5

COURSE
SNACK

COUSINE
AMERICAN

Commercially prepared beef jerky is commonly available in the market. But there is nothing as flavourful and delicious as homemade beef jerky. In this recipe, we will learn how to prepare beef jerky from scratch.

INGREDIENTS

- 1 ½ kg round beef steak
- ¼ cup honey
- ¼ cup soy sauce
- ¼ cup Worcestershire sauce
- ¼ cup brown sugar
- 2 tsp garlic powder
- 1 tbsp red pepper flakes
- 1 tsp salt
- 2 tsp onion powder

DIRECTIONS

1. First, prepare the beef by trimming the extra fat and skin from the meat.
2. Next, cut the meat into ¼ inch slices. Make sure that the slices are evenly cut.
3. Set the meat aside.
4. In a medium-size saucepan, add the honey, soy sauce, Worcestershire sauce, pepper, salt, garlic powder, onion powder, and sugar. Simmer it over the flame until a uniform mixture is formed.
5. Let the mixture reach room temperature. Apply the mixture generously on the beef slices and put them in a zip lock bag.
6. Pour the remaining sauce into the zip lock bag. Let it in the refrigerator overnight.
7. The next day, prepare the grill and turn it on with the maximum heat setting.
8. Meanwhile, please take out the beef slices and set them on a tray, and let them reach room temperature.
9. After that, arrange them in an aluminum tray and put them on the grill. Close the grill hood and let it grill for 3 hours.
10. Take it out after three hours and rest for about 2 to 3 hours until it becomes dry.
11. You can consume it as a snack and store it in an airtight container for up to 2 weeks.

6.12. Grilled Striped Bass

TOTAL TIME
3 HOURS

PREPARATION TIME
45'

COOK TIME
2 HOURS

SERVING
6

COURSE
LUNCH

COUSINE
AMERICAN

This is a delicious recipe having a mouth-watering flavor. Smoking the fish gives a much better flavor than just grilling. The smokiness makes this dish worth enjoying on a warm summer day. You can have it with a rich tartar sauce or a little lime juice drizzled on it. If you try this recipe, you are in for a treat.

INGREDIENTS

- 1 kg striped sea bass fillets
- ¼ cup brown sugar
- 4 cups water
- ¼ cup salt
- 2 bay leaves.
- 2 tsp black pepper
- 5 to 6 lemon slices
- ½ cup dry wine
- 3 tsp olive oil

DIRECTIONS

1. Clean and wash the fish fillets.
2. Heat the four cups of water and dissolve salt and sugar in them. Let it come to room temperature.
3. When it is at room temperature add, bay leaves, pepper, wine, and lemon slices.
4. Put in the fish fillets inside this brine such that they are completely soaked.
5. Cover them and leave them overnight.
6. The next day turn on the grill at medium heat settings.
7. Bring out the fish fillets and take them out of the brine and wash them with cold water. Set them on the counter on a tray lined with paper towels. Let them dry and come to room temperature.
8. Meanwhile, coat the grills with olive oil.
9. When the fish fillets have reached room temperature, set them on the grill for 5 minutes on each side.
10. Please take off the fish from the grill and let it rest for 10 minutes before serving.

101

6.13. Grilled Cajun Shrimp

TOTAL TIME
1 HOUR

PREPARATION TIME
20'

COOK TIME
30'

SERVING
6

COURSE
APPETIZER

COUSINE
AMERICAN

Shrimps are a crowd's favorite seafood. They are easy to make, and preparation also takes a few minutes. Either you are using fresh shrimps or frozen ones, this recipe works best for both. The only thing is that for frozen shrimps, you will have to defrost them first. This recipe is easy and simple to follow and seldom goes wrong. You will thank us when you have tried this one.

INGREDIENTS

- 1 kg jumbo shrimps
- ¼ cup salt
- 2 tbsp dried thyme
- 3 tbsp paprika
- 2 tsp cayenne pepper
- 2 tbsp onion powder
- 3 tbsp black pepper
- 2 tbsp garlic powder
- 3 tbsp olive oil
- ¼ cup lemon juice
- 1 bunch fresh parsley

DIRECTIONS

1. Prepare the shrimps. Take out the shells and devein them. Wash and pat them dry.
2. In a bowl, prepare the dry rum. Add salt, sugar, cayenne pepper, paprika, garlic powder, thyme, and onion powder. Mix this carefully.
3. Next, prepare an aluminum tray by greasing it with olive oil.
4. Place the shrimps on the tray in a single layer.
5. Apply the dry rum to the shrimps generously.
6. Let the grill preheat for 20 minutes.
7. Meanwhile, pour lemon juice over the shrimps.
8. Put the shrimps on the grill and close the hood.
9. Please take out the shrimps after 30 minutes or as soon as they start turning pink.
10. This dish can be served warmed or even at room temperature.

102

6.14. Grilled Scallops

TOTAL TIME
50'

PREPARATION TIME
5'

COOK TIME
30-40'

SERVING
5

COURSE
APPETIZER

COUSINE
AMERICAN

Scallops are juicy and delicious, either grilled or cooked. In this recipe, we have smoked the scallops to give them a rich smokiness. The scallops can be enjoyed with a side of a fresh green salad. This is the ultimate healthy dish to eat for lunch. Do try it out for a different and mouth-watering experience. You will not be disappointed.

INGREDIENTS

- 1 kg sea scallops
- 3 tbsp olive oil
- 1 tsp salt
- 2 garlic cloves minced.
- 1 tsp pepper

DIRECTIONS

1. Wash the scallops under cold running water and dry them on a paper towel.
2. In a bowl, mix the oil, salt, pepper, and lemon juice.
3. Apply the mixture to the scallops.
4. Turn on the grill for medium to high heat setting.
5. Meanwhile, lightly grease an aluminum pan and place the scallops on it such that the scallops do not touch each other.
6. Put the scallops on the grill and cover with the grill hood.
7. Let the scallops in the grill for 40 minutes, and then let them off the grill.
8. Let the scallops rest for 10 minutes and then serve with a fresh green salad and a vinaigrette.

6.15. Grilled Chicken Wings

TOTAL TIME
1H 50'

PREPARATION TIME
20'

COOK TIME
1H 30'

SERVING
4

COURSE
LUNCH

COUSINE
AMERICAN

Chicken wings are another crowd favorite. This recipe used a lot of spices and cut the overpowering spicy flavor; sugar is used. The sugar gives a sweet taste and a crispy finish with its caramelization. This is a perfect dish if you are planning to host a barbecue party.

INGREDIENTS

- 2.5 kg chicken wings
- 2 tsp salt
- 1 tsp pepper
- 1 tsp onion powder
- 1 tsp garlic powder
- ¼ cup paprika
- 1 tsp cayenne pepper
- ½ cup brown sugar

DIRECTIONS

1. Wash the chicken wings with cold water and trim them.
2. If you wish, you can break the wings in half or keep them full. Depends on your preference.
3. Next, mix the paprika, salt, pepper, onion powder, garlic powder, sugar, and cayenne pepper in a big mixing bowl.
4. Toss the chicken wings into this spice rub. Use your hands to coat the chicken wings with the spice rub.
5. Heat the grill and put the chicken wings on the grill.
6. Grill the wings for 7 to 8 minutes on each side and then take them off the grill in a platter.
7. Serve the delicious chicken wings immediately.

6.16. Herbal Chicken

TOTAL TIME
30'

PREPARATION TIME
10'

COOK TIME
20'

SERVING
4

COURSE
LUNCH

COUSINE
AMERICAN

This is a delicious recipe of chicken wings that has a strong flavor of herbs and spices. This recipe is inspired by French cuisine. Make this recipe to enjoy the Parisian feel in the comfort of your own house.

INGREDIENTS

- 2.5 kg chicken wings 2.5 kg
- ½ cup olive oil
- 2 garlic minced.
- 2 tbsp rosemary leaves
- 2 tbsp fresh basil leaves
- 2 tbsp lemon juice
- 1 ½ tsp salt
- 1 tsp pepper
- 2 tbsp oregano

DIRECTIONS

1. Prepare the chicken wings by trimming them. Wash the wings under cold running water.
2. It is your choice to break the wings into half or use them as it is.
3. In a large mixing bowl, add all ingredients and herbs and make a smooth mixture.
4. Save half and toss the chicken wings in the other half.
5. Use your hands to toss the wings in the mixture so that it is evenly applied.
6. Preheat the grill.
7. Arrange the chicken wings on the grill. Grill for 7 minutes on each side.
8. Check for doneness. The meat on the wings should be tender.
9. Take off the wings from the grill. Let them rest for 5 to 10 minutes before serving.

6.17. Grilled Redfish

TOTAL TIME
2H 10'

PREPARATION TIME
40'

COOK TIME
2 HOURS

SERVING
6

COURSE
LUNCH

COUSINE
AMERICAN

In this fish, we are using a dry brine technique. This is an easy and quick recipe; however, it requires the fish to marinate overnight. If you are planning to call guests over, you can prepare the fish fillets in advance.

INGREDIENTS

- 2 redfish fillets with skin 600g
- ½ cup salt
- 1 tsp black pepper
- 1 tsp lemon zest
- 1 tsp garlic powder 1tsp
- 2 slices of lemon

DIRECTIONS

1. Wash the fish fillets with cold running water.
2. Next, prepare a rub by mixing all the ingredients and spices.
3. Apply the rub on the fish fillets generously. Wrap the fish fillets in cling film and refrigerate them overnight.
4. The next day takes out the fish fillets and brings them to room temperature.
5. Prepare the grill. Preheat it to a medium heat level.
6. When the fillets are at room temperature, wash them and pat them dry.
7. Put them in aluminum foil and place them on the grill.
8. Frill for 1 hour and keep flipping the fish occasionally.
9. After 1 hour, take the fish off the grill and then unwrap the foil.
10. Let the fillets rest for 30 minutes before serving.

6.18. Grilled Dory

TOTAL TIME
1H 15'

PREPARATION TIME
15'

COOK TIME
1 HOUR

SERVING
4

COURSE
DINNER

COUSINE
AMERICAN

This fish is easy to cook and quickly prepared. We will use the dry rub method to prepare the dory fish fillets. This turns out to be a delicious recipe and is a crowd favorite.

INGREDIENTS

- 4 fillets of dory
- 1 tsp onion Powder
- ½ cup salt
- 2 tsp black pepper
- 1 tsp ginger powder
- 1 tsp garlic powder
- Coriander for garnish
- Lemon slices for garnish

DIRECTIONS

1. Wash the fish fillets with cold running water.
2. Next, prepare a rub by mixing all the ingredients and spices.
3. Apply the rub on the fish fillets generously. Wrap the fish fillets in cling film and refrigerate them overnight.
4. The next day takes out the fish fillets and brings them to room temperature.
5. Prepare the electric Smoker with wood chips and water. Turn it on at 2200F.
6. When the fillets are at room temperature, wash them and pat them dry.
7. Preheat the grill.
8. Grill the fish fillets for 4 minutes on each side.
9. Let the fillets rest for 30 minutes before serving.
10. Garnish the fish fillets with coriander and lemon slices for serving.

6.19. Grilled Herbal Salmon

TOTAL TIME
1 HOUR

PREPARATION TIME
45'

COOK TIME
15'

SERVING
6

COURSE
DINNER

COUSINE
AMERICAN

Salmon is one fish variety that is consumed very often among people. The reason for this is that it is an excellent source of protein, and it cooks easily. Smoked salmon is something that you can enjoy at family dinners and other gatherings. You can never go wrong with smoked salmon.

INGREDIENTS

- 750 g Salmon fillets
- ¼ cup salt
- ¼ cup sugar
- ½ cup water
- 2 tbsp black pepper
- 2 slices lemon
- 1 bunch fresh dill

DIRECTIONS

1. Prepare the marinade for the fish. In a flat dish, pour water, salt, sugar, and pepper. Mix them well.
2. Soak the fish fillets in the marinade and cover them with dill and lemon slices.
3. Wrap the fillets in cling wrap and refrigerate overnight.
4. The next day, take out the fish fillets, remove the cling wrap, and bring them to room temperature.
5. Preheat the grill.
6. Grill the fish fillets for 4 minutes on each side.
7. Take off from the grill and let it rest for 5 minutes before serving.

6.20. Grilled Chicken

TOTAL TIME
50'

PREPARATION TIME
20'

COOK TIME
30'

SERVING
4

COURSE
DINNER

COUSINE
AMERICAN

This is a simple recipe and can never go wrong. Easy to make and delicious to taste. You can prepare this overnight and smoke it the next day. Family and friends will enjoy it alike.

INGREDIENTS

- 1 kg chicken breast pieces
- 2 tsp black pepper
- 2 tsp salt
- 4 tbsp lemon juice
- 2 tbsp paprika

DIRECTIONS

1. Wash the chicken breast pieces. It is your choice to remove the skin or keep it.
2. Pat the chicken dry.
3. In a flat dish, mix the salt, pepper, paprika, and lemon juice.
4. Apply the mixture generously on the chicken and wrap the pieces with cling wrap and leave it in the refrigerator overnight.
5. The next day, take out the chicken from the fridge and let it warm up to room temperature.
6. Wash the chicken fillets under cold water.
7. Pat, the chicken, dries with paper towels.
8. Now, preheat the grill. Grill the chicken fillets on the grill.
9. Grill the chicken for 7 minutes on each side.
10. Take the chicken from the grill and serve with your choice of sides.

6.21. Sweet Grilled Salmon

TOTAL TIME
1 HOUR

PREPARATION TIME
10'

COOK TIME
50'

SERVING
4

COURSE
LUNCH

COUSINE
AMERICAN

This is an easy and delicious fish recipe. Salmon is a variety of famous fish among people, and a lot of people enjoy it. This grilled fish recipe is delicious and is rich in protein. It would help if you tried this recipe, and you will not be disappointed.

INGREDIENTS

- 300g salmon
- ¼ cup maple syrup
- ¼ teaspoon pepper
- 2 ½ tablespoon soy sauce
- 2 clove garlic chopped
- ½ teaspoon garlic powder

DIRECTIONS

1. Preheat the grill.
2. Mix the garlic, soy sauce, maple syrup, garlic salt, and pepper in a small bowl.
3. Put the fish in an oven-safe glass dish and pour the maple mixture on it. Rub the mixture on the fish so that it is fully coated.
4. Put a cling wrap on the dish and marinate the fish for 20 minutes in the fridge. After 20 minutes, turn the fish and cover it again. Let it marinate for 20 more minutes.
5. Take out the baking dish from the fridge and take off cling wrap.
6. Now wrap the fish in aluminum foil.
7. Put the fish on the grill and cover the grill with the cover.
8. Grill the fish for 50 minutes and keep flipping them occasionally.
9. Remove the aluminum foil and put it on the serving plate.
10. Check for doneness with a fork. If a fork easily flakes the fish, it means it is done.

6.22. Grilled Okra

TOTAL TIME
20'

PREPARATION TIME
10'

COOK TIME
10'

SERVING
4

COURSE
DINNER

COUSINE
AMERICAN

Okra is one of the vegetables which is a favorite among people. This recipe gives okra a new dimension. The crunchy texture that the okra gets makes it a beautiful experience. Try this recipe, and you will not regret it.

INGREDIENTS

- 500g okra
- ½ teaspoon garlic powder
- ¼ teaspoon ground black pepper
- 2 teaspoon olive oil
- ½ cup cornmeal
- ½ cup breadcrumbs

DIRECTIONS

1. First, preheat the grill on a low to medium heat setting.
2. Prepare a tray. Wash okra and pat dry. Spread on the tray in a single layer.
3. The drying is critical. If any moisture is left, the okra can taste soggy rather than crunchy.
4. Slit the okra in the centre without fully cutting it.
5. In a large bowl, add garlic powder, pepper, cornmeal, breadcrumbs, and pepper.
6. Fill this breadcrumb filling in the slit okra.
7. Brush the okra with olive oil.
8. Grill the vegetable for 5 to 7 minutes with flipping and turning occasionally.
9. Take off from the grill and serve immediately while it is crunchy.

6.23. Grilled Tuna and Broccoli Pasta

TOTAL TIME
1H 15'

PREPARATION TIME
45'

COOK TIME
30'

SERVING
6-8

COURSE
LUNCH

COUSINE
AMERICAN

Seafood and fish are a great source of protein and should be included in your diet. This pasta also includes broccoli which is a source of protein and is good for your overall health. Try out this easy recipe, and you will not regret it.

INGREDIENTS

- 400g tuna fish fillets
- 500g macaroni
- 250g broccoli chopped
- 2 tablespoon flour
- 3 slices sourdough bread
- 500ml milk
- 2 red onions, finely chopped

- 4 tablespoon vinegar
- 50g butter
- 2 tablespoon mustard
- 250g cheddar cheese
- 2 tablespoon capers
- 3 tablespoon chopped parsley

DIRECTIONS

1. Heat the grill at medium heat level.
2. Wash the tuna fillets and rub some olive oil on them. Season with salt and freshly ground pepper.
3. Grill the tuna on the grill for 4 to 7 minutes on each side. Take care that the fish is not burnt.
4. Set aside on a cutting board.
5. Cut into thick slices and set aside.
6. Meanwhile, preheat the oven at 3000F.
7. Mix onion and vinegar in a small bowl. Set aside.
8. Cook pasta for 8 minutes in boiling water. Drain the water and set pasta aside.
9. Put broccoli in a steamer and steam for five minutes.
10. Prepare the white sauce. Take a large saucepan, melt the butter. Add the flour slowly and mix. No lumps should be formed. Cook for at least two minutes.
11. Turn off the heat and add milk gradually and mix well. Take care that no lumps are formed.
12. Turn on the heat and cook on a high flame for two minutes.
13. Turn off the heat and add the mustard and cheese and mix till the cheese melts.
14. To this sauce, add the pasta and broccoli and half of the parsley. Drain the vinegar from the onion and add the onion to the white sauce.
15. Put all of this in a large oven-safe dish.
16. Scatter some sourdough pieces on the top of the dish.
17. Bake for 30 minutes.
18. The dish will be bubbly after taking out of the oven. Wait for it to stop bubbling.
19. Serve the pasta with grilled tuna on the side.
20. Serve immediately

6.24. Grilled Garlic Chicken

TOTAL TIME
55'

PREPARATION TIME
10'

COOK TIME
45'

SERVING
4

COURSE
LUNCH

COUSINE
SOUTH ASIAN

This is an amazing recipe, and you can have it for lunch or dinner. The chicken is tender, and the flavor of garlic enhances the whole dish. The sweet flavor of honey gives it a different dimension, and it is a good change from the usual chicken dishes we eat.

INGREDIENTS

- 1kg chicken thighs
- 1 tablespoon olive oil
- 2 tablespoons honey
- 2 tablespoon garlic paste
- 3 tablespoons honey
- 1 teaspoon cayenne pepper
- Salt to taste

DIRECTIONS

1. First, preheat the grill to a high heat setting.
2. Wash and clean chicken drumsticks. Dry them with a paper towel.
3. Make diagonal cuts on the chicken meat. Two cuts on each drumstick. This will make sure that the marinade will impart flavor throughout the chicken.
4. Put chicken thighs in a baking pan.
5. Rub olive oil on the chicken.
6. Next, rub garlic paste on the chicken. Rub some into the slits as well.
7. Mix salt and cayenne pepper with honey and pour over the chicken. Rub the honey pic on the chicken and to the slits as well.
8. Cover the chicken with aluminum foil and grill for 20 minutes. Keep flipping occasionally so that the heat is evenly distributed.
9. Take out the chicken, remove the aluminum foil, and again grill for about 4 minutes on each side so that grill marks can be formed and the chicken is thoroughly cooked.
10. Serve hot.

6.25. Grilled Cod Fish

TOTAL TIME
15'

PREPARATION TIME
5'

COOK TIME
10'

SERVING
1-2

COURSE
DINNER

COUSINE
AMERICAN

Fish is a great source of protein, and codfish is delicious. Try this mouth-watering recipe, and you will not be disappointed. You can enjoy the codfish as it is or with a side of grilled vegetables. Once you try this dish, this will become a regular in your home menu.

INGREDIENTS

- 2 cod fish fillets
- 2 tablespoon lemon juice
- 2 tablespoons oil
- 1 tablespoon chopped parsley
- 2 tablespoon lemon juice
- ½ teaspoon cayenne pepper
- Salt to taste

DIRECTIONS

1. First, preheat the grill for a medium heat setting.
2. Rinse the fish fillets with cold water and pat dry with a paper towel.
3. Put all the fish fillets on a dish.
4. In a small bowl, add lemon juice, salt, and cayenne pepper. Pour this over the fish and rub a little.
5. Grill the fish fillets for 4 minutes on each side and take them out on a serving platter.
6. Check for doneness. Use a fork to check if the fish easily flakes. It means it is done.
7. Top with fresh parsley.
8. Serve hot.

6.26. Grilled Fish Fillet

TOTAL TIME
20'

PREPARATION TIME
10'

COOK TIME
10'

SERVING
4

COURSE
LUNCH

COUSINE
AMERICAN

This is an amazing recipe, and you can have it for lunch or dinner. The chicken is tender, and the flavor of garlic enhances the whole dish. The sweet flavor of honey gives it a different dimension, and it is a good change from the usual chicken dishes we eat.

INGREDIENTS

- 4 fillets (medium size) of tilapia fish
- 3 cloves garlic chopped
- ½ cup Parmesan cheese
- 2 tablespoon chopped parsley
- 2 tablespoons freshly squeezed lemon juice
- 2 tablespoons olive oil
- 1 lemon cut in wedges
- ½ teaspoon cayenne pepper
- ½ teaspoon pepper
- salt to taste

DIRECTIONS

1. First, preheat the grill at a medium heat setting.
2. Wash the fish fillets water and dry with a paper towel.
3. Put all the fish fillets in the baking dish.
4. In a small bowl, mix garlic, cayenne pepper, salt, olive oil, black pepper, and lemon juice. Pour this over the fish fillets.
5. Now grill the fish fillets on the grill. Fish usually takes less time to grill. Grill each side for 3 to 4 minutes and then take off from the grill into a serving platter.
6. Top the fish fillets with parmesan cheese and fresh parsley.
7. Serve hot with fresh lemon slices.

6.27. Grilled Pepper and Spinach Pasta

TOTAL TIME
1 HOUR

PREPARATION TIME
40'

COOK TIME
20'

SERVING
4-6

COURSE
DINNER

COUSINE
AMERICAN

Leafy greens are always recommended for good health and a great source of vitamins. This is a healthy option for lunch as well as dinner. This recipe is easy to follow and delicious to make. Make this recipe, and you will not regret it.

INGREDIENTS

- 200g spinach
- 400g red bell pepper cut into thick strips
- 400g penne pasta
- 500g store-bought tomato pasta sauce
- 100g goat cheese grated
- 30g raisins
- 2 tablespoon olive oil
- 1 teaspoon dry thyme
- 2 onions sliced
- 2 garlic cloves chopped
- 1 teaspoon chili flakes
- 1 tablespoon sugar

DIRECTIONS

1. First, preheat the oven to 300°F.
2. Prepare the pasta by cooking it in boiling water for 8 minutes.
3. Remove the water and set aside the pasta.
4. In a separate frying pan, heat some oil and add the onions. Cook for five minutes till the onions start to soften.
5. Add garlic and stir for one minute. After that, add the pepper strips. In the end, add the chili flakes. Cook on a high flame for one minute.
6. Next, add tomato sauce, raisins, spinach, thyme, and sugar. Keep stirring and cook for 10 minutes on medium flame.
7. Put in the pasta and mix well.
8. Next, pour all the pasta into an aluminum dish. Cover it with aluminum foil.
9. Put the dish in the grill and cover it with the grill cover.
10. Let the pasta grill for 20 minutes till the liquid inside starts bubbling.
11. Take out the dish from the grill and wait for the bubbling to finish before opening the aluminum covering from the top.
12. Serve warm.

6.28. Grilled Pepper Beef

TOTAL TIME
5H 30'

PREPARATION TIME
4 HOURS

COOK TIME
1H 30'

SERVING
1-2

COURSE
DINNER

COUSINE
AMERICAN

Beef and pepper go together really well. This is an amazing recipe which you can serve your family and friends. This is a rich recipe, and the aromatic flavor makes you prepare it again and again. This is an easy and simple recipe, and you will not be disappointed if you try it.

INGREDIENTS

- 3kg beef
- 2 tablespoon coarse pepper
- ¾ cup horseradish grated
- 2 tablespoon sugar
- Salt to taste.

DIRECTIONS

1. Obtain a large piece of beef meat without the bone. Tie it to form a loaf shape.
2. In a small bowl, mix salt and sugar. Rub the beef with this mixture.
3. Line a deep baking dish with aluminum foil and place the beef on it. Cover with cling wrap and chill for 3 hours in the fridge.
4. Take out the beef after three hours. Remove the cling wrap.
5. In a small bowl, mix salt, pepper, and horseradish. Pat horseradish mixture over the top and sides of beef.
6. Heat up the grill.
7. Cover the beef with aluminum foil completely and place it on the grill. Cover it with the grill cover.
8. Let it grill for 1 hour and 30 minutes, flipping it occasionally.
9. Take out from the grill and remove the aluminum foil.
10. Let it rest for 10 minutes.
11. Next, cut into thin slices.
12. Save the juices released while grilling and pour over the meat slices for flavor.
13. Serve warm. Enjoy your meal.

6.29. Grilled Beef Teriyaki

TOTAL TIME
5 HOURS

PREPARATION TIME
3-4 HOURS

COOK TIME
45'

SERVING
2-4

COURSE
LUNCH

COUSINE
AMERICAN

Another delicious recipe that makes sure that all the flavor notes are perfect. The teriyaki sauce makes it even more mouth-watering. This is packed with protein and a good energy source. If you try this recipe once, you will want to grill it again and again.

INGREDIENTS

- 1 ½ kg beef steak
- 2 tablespoon garlic (chopped)
- 1 cup potato (diced)
- 1 cup store-bought teriyaki marinade
- 1 onion sliced
- 1 carrot sliced
- 2 tablespoon olive oil.
- ½ teaspoon black pepper

DIRECTIONS

1. Cut the beef into strips. Remove as much fat as possible.
2. Rub the beef with garlic.
3. In a large bowl, mix the potatoes, carrots, onions, and beef. Pour the teriyaki marinade and olive oil. Coat all the ingredients with marinade.
4. Leave to marinate for 4 hours.
5. Heat up the grill to maximum heat level.
6. Meanwhile, prepare an aluminum dish. Put all the beef and marinade in the dish and cover it with aluminum foil. By covering it with aluminum foil.
7. Put the dish on the grill and cover it with the grill cover. Let it grill for 45 mins to 1 hour.
8. Check if the beef is tender.
9. Serve warm.

6.30. Grilled Chicken Teriyaki

TOTAL TIME
5 HOURS

PREPARATION TIME
3-4 HOURS

COOK TIME
45'

SERVING
2-4

COURSE
DINNER

COUSINE
AMERICAN

INGREDIENTS

- 1 ½ kg chicken steak
- 2 tablespoon garlic (chopped)
- 1 cup potato (diced)
- 1 cup store-bought teriyaki marinade
- 1 onion sliced
- 1 carrot sliced
- 2 tablespoon olive oil.
- ½ teaspoon black pepper

DIRECTIONS

1. Cut the chicken into strips. Remove as much fat as possible.
2. Rub the chicken with garlic.
3. In a large bowl, mix the potatoes, carrots, onions, and beef. Pour the teriyaki marinade and olive oil. Coat all the ingredients with marinade.
4. Leave to marinate for 4 hours.
5. Preheat the grill for a high heat setting.
6. Meanwhile, prepare the aluminum dish and put all the beef and marinade in the dish. Cover it with aluminum foil.
7. Put the dish on the grill and cover it with a grill cover. Grill for 45 minutes.
8. After 45 minutes, check if the chicken is tender.
9. Serve warm.

6.31. Grilled Seabass

TOTAL TIME
30'

PREPARATION TIME
10'

COOK TIME
20'

SERVING
2-3

COURSE
LUNCH

COUSINE
AMERICAN

INGREDIENTS

- 750g sea bass
- ¾ tablespoon sesame oil
- 2 clove garlic sliced
- 2 green onions
- 2 tablespoon ginger slices
- 1 ½ soy sauce
- ½ tbsp rice vinegar

DIRECTIONS

1. First, heat up the grill for a medium to high heat setting.
2. Snip the corners of the spring onions and peel off the rough outer layer (both dark green and stem). Break them into 5-7 cm (approximately 2-3 inch) bits and cut them by the length in half. Slice the ginger into thin strips and peel and chop the garlic into small pieces.
3. Cover a baking dish wide enough to accommodate the fish with a sheet of aluminum foil that is large enough to fold the fish together with a little extra. Spread a layer of onion, ginger, and garlic at the bottom of the foil.
4. Create two cuts on each side of the sea bass, then put them on top of the onion, garlic, and ginger slices.
5. Place in the dish a few more bits of onion, ginger, and garlic, then place the few slices of garlic and ginger into the slits on the side of the fish.
6. One onion should still be remaining.
7. Combine the soya sauce, rice vinegar, and sesame oil and spread over the fish. To close up the package, wrap the fish into the foil and secure it on the edges by folding.
8. Grill the fish while wrapped in the aluminum foil. Turn it and flip it after every 5 to 6 minutes. Grill for 20 minutes.
9. Check for doneness. The fish should be thoroughly done.
10. Serve hot, topped with the remaining onion.

6.32. Grilled Chicken and Lettuce Wrap

TOTAL TIME
15'

PREPARATION TIME
5'

COOK TIME
10'

SERVING
1

COURSE
DINNER

COUSINE
AMERICAN

This is a healthy option if you are avoiding carbohydrates or a gluten-free diet. This is a great source of protein and vitamins. This dish is easy to prepare and delicious in flavor and taste. Try this recipe, and you will not be disappointed.

INGREDIENTS

- 2 whole iceberg lettuce leaves
- 100g chicken cubed.
- 1 tbsp olive oil
- 1 tbsp mustard
- 2 tsp lemon juice
- 15 g chopped cilantro
- 25 g chopped green onion
- 1 garlic clove minced
- 1 small carrot chopped
- 1 tsp chili flakes

DIRECTIONS

1. Chill the lettuce leaves in the freezer for 10 minutes.
2. Meanwhile, cook the chicken cubes in 1 tbsp oil for 10-15 mins on low flame.
3. Put the cooked chicken in a bowl, mix all the remaining ingredients except for the lettuce leaves.
4. On a plate, set the lettuce leaves side by side and spoon the mixture onto the leaves.
5. Wrap the lettuce leaves.
6. Heat up the grill and grill the lettuce wraps for 2 to 3 minutes.
7. Enjoy your grilled lettuce wraps.

6.33. Fish Tacos

TOTAL TIME
20'

PREPARATION TIME
10'

COOK TIME
30'

SERVING
1

COURSE
LUNCH

COUSINE
MEXICAN

Fish and seafood are a great option for good quality protein. This yummy recipe of tacos ensures good flavor and health together. Once you prepare this recipe, you will be making it repeatedly to experience the great flavors.

INGREDIENTS

- 100 g boneless fish
- 1 small onion sliced.
- 3 tbsp ranch
- 1 small tomato sliced.
- 100 g lettuce chopped.
- 2 soft shell tacos
- ½ tsp salt
- ½ tsp pepper
- 2 tbsp oil to fry
- 100 g grated cheese

DIRECTIONS

1. In a frying pan, fry fish in oil and add salt and pepper. Cook for 5 minutes and then take out on a plate.
2. Now assemble the tocos by putting, lettuce, then fish, then tomatoes and onions.
3. Top with grated cheese and fold the toco.
4. Brush olive oil lightly on the outer side of the tocos.
5. Heat up the grill and grill the tocos for 2 minutes on each side.
6. You will get warm toasty tocos with melted cheese.
7. Enjoy your meal.

6.34 Chicken Tacos

TOTAL TIME
20'

PREPARATION TIME
10'

COOK TIME
30'

SERVING
1

COURSE
DINNER

COUSINE
MEXICAN

This is a recipe for delicious tacos. The chicken is tender and melts in your mouth. The cheesy flavor makes it rich and delicious. This is amazing comfort food.

INGREDIENTS

- 100 g boneless chicken breast
- 1 small onion sliced.
- 3 tbsp
- 2 tbsp ranch
- 1 small tomato sliced.
- 100 g lettuce chopped.
- 2 soft shell tacos
- ½ tsp salt
- ½ tsp pepper
- 3 tbsp oil to fry
- 100 g grated cheese

DIRECTIONS

1. Cut the chicken breast into small pieces.
2. In a frying pan, fry chicken in oil and add salt and pepper. Cook for 10 minutes and then take out on a plate.
3. Now assemble the tacos by putting, lettuce, then fish, then tomatoes and onions.
4. Top with grated cheese and fold the taco. Brush a little bit of olive oil on the tacos.
5. Heat up the grill and grill the tacos for 2 minutes on each side.
6. Serve the tacos warm and toasty.
7. Enjoy your meal.

6.35 Prawn Tacos

TOTAL TIME
20'

PREPARATION TIME
10'

COOK TIME
30'

SERVING
2

COURSE
DINNER

COUSINE
MEXICAN

Tacos are a famous Mexican dish popular throughout the world. They are easy to make and delicious to eat. The filling can be of your choice. The tangy sauce in the tacos makes the flavor mouth-watering and delicious at the same time.

INGREDIENTS

- 100 g prawns
- 1 small onion sliced.
- 3 tbsp ranch
- 1 small tomato sliced.
- 100 g lettuce chopped.
- 2 soft shell tacos
- ½ tsp salt
- ½ tsp pepper
- 3 tbsp oil to fry
- 100 g grated cheese

DIRECTIONS

1. Peel the skin off the prawns and devein them. Wash them with cold water.
2. In a frying pan, fry prawns in oil and add salt and pepper. Cook for 3 minutes and then take out on a plate.
3. Now assemble the tacos by putting, lettuce, then fish, then tomatoes and onions.
4. Top with grated cheese and fold the taco.
5. Heat the grill and grill the tacos on the heated grill. Grill for 2 minutes on both sides.
6. Serve when warm and toasty.

6.36 Grilled Chicken with Rice

TOTAL TIME
45'

PREPARATION TIME
10'

COOK TIME
35'

SERVING
2

COURSE
DINNER

COUSINE
AMERICAN

This is a basic dinner recipe. The chicken is delicious and high in protein content. The chili in the recipe makes it spicy and delicious. This dish is packed with protein and is good for both dinner and lunch.

INGREDIENTS

- 200 g chicken breast
- 2 tbsp ginger thinly sliced.
- 5 green chilis sliced longitudinally.
- ½ tsp salt
- ½ tsp pepper
- 2tbsp vinegar
- 2 tbsp soy sauce
- 1 tbsp chili sauce
- 2 tbsp olive oil

DIRECTIONS

1. Preheat the grill for medium to high heat setting.
2. Rub the chicken with olive oil and season with salt.
3. Grill the chicken breast. t does not take very long to grill chicken. Grill chicken for 5 minutes on each side and let it rest before slicing.
4. After 5 minutes, slice the chicken into thin strips.
5. In a mixing bowl, add chicken with vinegar, soy sauce, chili sauce, salt, and pepper. Put this mixture in a pan and flame for 2 minutes, and take it out on a plate.
6. Garnish with ginger and green chili.
7. Serve warm with boiled rice.

6.37 Chicken Burgers

TOTAL TIME
30'

PREPARATION TIME
10'

COOK TIME
20'

SERVING
2

COURSE
LUNCH

COUSINE
AMERICAN

A lot of people prefer chicken burgers. The reason being that chicken can be cooked quickly and easily. Chicken patties can be easily cooked within half the time of any other meat patties. Enjoy this simple and easy-to-follow recipe for delicious burgers.

INGREDIENTS

- 100 g chicken mince
- ½ tsp salt
- ½ tsp curry powder
- 2 tbsp chopped coriander
- 2 tbsp chopped onion
- 2 tbsp chopped tomato
- 1 tsp oil
- 2 burger buns

DIRECTIONS

1. In a large mixing bowl, add the chicken mince. Mix all the ingredients except the oil. Mix well.
2. Now make two thick burger patties.
3. Coat the patties with olive oil.
4. Heat up the grill and put the burger patties on the grill. It does not take long for chicken patties to cook. Grill for 4 minutes on each side and then take off from the grill.
5. Set them in the burger bun and enjoy with tomato ketchup.

6.38 Beef Burgers

TOTAL TIME
30'

PREPARATION TIME
10'

COOK TIME
20'

SERVING
2

COURSE
LUNCH

COUSINE
AMERICAN

Burgers are popular among people. You will find someone grilling burgers at all family grilling sessions. One reason is that burgers are easy to prepare and delicious to eat. Keeping this in mind, we have included this simple burger recipe. The hope is that you will enjoy this recipe.

INGREDIENTS

- 100 g chicken mince
- ½ tsp salt
- ½ tsp curry powder
- 2 tbsp chopped coriander
- 2 tbsp chopped onion
- 2 tbsp chopped tomato
- Oil to fry
- 2 burger buns

DIRECTIONS

1. In a large mixing bowl, add the chicken mince. Mix all the ingredients except the oil. Mix well.
2. Now make two thick burger patties.
3. Grill the burger patties. Beef usually takes longer. It will take around 7 to 8 minutes on each side. Be sure that the patties are fully cooked and then take off from the grill.
4. Arrange them in the burger bun and enjoy with tomato ketchup.

127

CONCLUSION

Grilling is a favorite activity throughout the United States of America and all over the world. Each culture has its barbecue traditions. Everyone enjoys sitting in their backyards and having family over, grilling, eating, and having good fun. This book is all about celebrating this excellent cooking method and an ode to beautiful family and friend gatherings.

Towards the end of the book, you must be feeling confident about your very first grilling experience. If you are always looking to improve your skills, this book must have indeed given you some great tips and delicious recipes. Cooking is all about perfecting your technique. Learning never stops. There was a time when you could only find eat recipes for the grill, and no vegetarian options were available. A lot of veggie and food lovers had to learn to grill their beloved vegetables by themselves. But not in this book, this book has given you a complete guide to deal with your delicate food item along with some delicious recipes for you to follow. The recipes included are carefully selected and are included with a step-by-step approach for easy understanding. The preparation and cooking times of individual recipes are mentioned to choose your recipes according to the time you have. However, it is always suggested that while grilling, you must have some extra time on hand as there are always chances of accidents as grilling is pretty unpredictable. Even the most seasoned people who have spent hours and hours near the grill sometimes go wrong. It never hurts to have a bit extra preparation, which is at least thirty minutes.

The hope was to provide you with the book that will make your journey towards grilling simple and make you fall in love with the art of cooking and grilling food. All skills are like art. Cooking is no exception to this, cooking is also an art. And by that, grilling is an art form. The more you practice, the more you will become perfect in your craft. Always remember, practice is the key. In cooking you will never achieve perfection in the first attempt. You will have to be very patient to achieve perfection.

129

RECIPE INDEX

Made in the USA
Monee, IL
31 July 2025

22232172R00072